Information Retrieval

Other Books in this Series

Aldus Science and Technology Series

Information Retrieval
The Essential Technology

Roger Meetham

 Aldus Books London

Design: **Roger Hyde**
Assistant: **Prudence Baldwin**
Research: **Julia Blackburn**
Diagrams: **Rudolph Britto,**
            Gillian Stagg

SBN:490 00133 5 (hard cover)
SBN:490 00134 3 (paperback)

First published in the United Kingdom by
Aldus Books Limited, Aldus House, 17, Conway Street, London, W.1.
Printed in Italy by Arnoldo Mondadori, Verona
Copyright © Aldus Books Limited, London, 1969

Contents

1 Communication and Memory

"All the nervous tissue of the beehive is the nervous tissue of some single bee: how then does the beehive act in unison, and at that in a very variable, adapted, organized unison? Obviously the secret is in the intercommunication of its members." These rather extravagant words of Norbert Wiener, the American pioneer of communication science, draw attention to the real reason why the human race has so completely outstripped the other animals in its development. Our manual dexterity, use of tools, and adaptability to unfavorable environments may have saved us from extinction in the very early days, but how did we come to multiply and spread over the face of the earth? It must have been chiefly because we spent most of our lives chattering to one another, and because of the variety of things we were able to chatter about. Communication is the real stuff of progress, of evolution; even science and technology are subservient to it and always have been.

Consider the sort of event that must have occurred thousands of times in the course of prehistory. A genius in some tribe

The worker honeybees in this photograph are in communication with the queen bee by receiving "queen substance." This and other substances are passed on to all members of the colony, informing them that their queen is well and present in the hive. This chapter considers similar examples in animal and human experience and describes how we can define and measure the information communicated.

discovers that he can throw a stone twice as hard by whirling it around his head in a sling and letting it go with a simple releasing device. He may keep the secret for a while, but the rest of his tribe will soon take to the invention and develop it. Other groups will notice how efficient this tribe is at hunting, and how powerful in battle. Their spies and their wise men will confer, and soon everybody will be fashioning slings and practicing the art of slinging. The invention will spread over the land with the proverbial speed of the grapevine. Without all this commotion and communication, the fate of the invention would be very different, and it would be lost at the death of its discoverer. Indeed it would never be discovered at all, because we can be sure that the genius does not start absolutely from scratch—he incorporates in his work a great deal of basic knowledge that has been communicated to him from his fellows, from his family, and indirectly from his ancestors.

In the last 30 years a new attitude to communication has been emerging, and it is best expressed by the word *cybernetics*, which was coined by a group of Americans, including Norbert Wiener, whose book of that title was published in 1948. Cybernetics is the study of "control and communication in the animal and the machine." It reminds us that communication is not just a matter of words going to and fro, or even the very numerous different representations of words. There are communications, for example, within the human body. These are mostly, though not all, in the nervous system and they govern the whole of our behavior. Any act of behavior is itself in some sense a communication—usually between people, but it may be within a person or between a person and a machine. Waving a handkerchief is a communication, scratching one's head, pressing a switch, and so on, almost without end. We shall in this book be concerned with communications for particular purposes, and the word *cybernetics* will not appear very often, because it is too general to be of help.

On the role of communication within a community, Wiener has much to say. He notices that a group may have more or less information than its members, depending on how much they have told each other, but even if the former is true, "not all the information which is available to the race at one time is accessible without special effort. There is a well-known tendency of libraries to become clogged by their own volume; of the sciences to develop such a degree of specialization that the expert is often illiterate outside his own minute speciality." It is opinions like this, of course, that have stimulated the present world-wide efforts to improve scientific communication and technological information retrieval.

Wiener also considers whether different sorts of community are *homeostatic* (that is, whether they have a relatively stable state of equilibrium) or whether they are such that the rich and strong become richer and stronger while the poor and weak become poorer and weaker. He observes that small, closely knit human communities have a very considerable measure of homeostasis, whether they are highly literate communities in a civilized country or villages of primitive savages. He goes on, "It is only in the large community, where the Lords of Things as They Are protect themselves from hunger by wealth, from public opinion by privacy and anonymity, from private criticism by the laws of libel and the possession of the means of communication, that ruthlessness can reach its most sublime levels. Of all these anti-homeostatic factors in society, the control of the means of communication is the most effective and the most important."

These words no doubt reflected the western world's recent escape from national socialism, and Wiener's own struggles as a Jew and an infant prodigy to gain acceptance by a society with some prejudices and an academic world of some exclusiveness. However, they imply—so long as a modicum of homeostasis is considered to be a worthwhile goal—that we are doomed unless we develop more universal communication and more efficient information retrieval. To do this, information and its storage and retrieval must be studied systematically. In this chapter we shall take a quick look at the very valuable concept of information and how we ordinarily transmit, receive, and retain it, before concentrating in the rest of the book on specific information storage and retrieval systems designed by man for his own use.

Information Theory

Before this almost too pervasive idea of communication gets out of hand, let us quickly examine how the mathematicians and engineers have pinned it down. In principle they have pinned it down completely, by definition and measurement, and their work now has applications in psychology and tele-communications. Moreover, by showing that it can be measured, the philosophers among these practical men have provided an important clarification of ideas and a safeguard against loose reasoning, especially in sociology and economics.

What they have pondered over is not communication itself, so much as what is communicated, and this they call *information*. The unit of information is called the *bit*, a con-tracted form of *binary digit*, and, as we shall see, it corresponds roughly to choosing between yes and no. When the prisoner in the dock, in answer to the inevitable question, says, "I plead not guilty," he is handing out one bit of information, to the court, the reporters, and the world at large. He could have said only one other thing, and I am pretending that nothing was previously known about him to indicate whether he would plead guilty or not guilty. Though we are here using the bit as a unit, we must not suppose there is too close a connection with the binary arithmetic of computers or with the idea of a binary choice. If the prisoner had been allowed a third reply, such as, "I refuse to plead," the information he gave could still be measured, but it would be necessary to know the probability of each of the three replies. We shall shortly be discussing the importance of probabilities in the measurement of information.

Although the bit is very small, there can easily be fractions of a bit. When the bridegroom in the church, in answer to another famous question, says, "I will," he is giving out very little information indeed, because everyone is pretty sure what his answer is going to be. Supposing, however, that experience shows about one bridegroom in a million will say, "I won't," the present one, in what must seem to him a very momentous statement, is yielding only 0.0000016 bit. But if he should decide to call the whole thing off, his "I won't" would be worth about

A bridegroom who says, "I won't" communicates about 20 bits of information and is worth a mention in most of the Sunday newspapers.

20 bits and a mention in most of the Sunday papers.

The above example indicates that information is largely connected with probability, but not in direct proportion. The two numerical answers of 0.0000016 bit and 20 bits were arrived at by using a formula devised by C. E. Shannon, who did much of the original work on information theory at the Bell Telephone Laboratories, New Jersey, in the 1940s. The basic definition of quantity of information runs as follows: *when a decision is announced, it conveys a quantity of information,*

$$-I = \log_2 p \text{ bits}$$

where p is the probability of that decision. I stands for information and $\log_2$ represents logarithm to the base 2. This means that 2 must be raised to the power $(-I)$ to equal p, or we can get rid of the minus sign and write $1/2^I = p$. In the example of the bridegroom. we suppose that the probability of his saying,

OVER										
1 METER?	NO	0								
$\frac{1}{2}$ METER?	YES		1							
$\frac{3}{4}$ METER?	NO			0						
$\frac{5}{8}$ METER?	YES				1					
$\frac{11}{16}$ METER?	YES					1				
$\frac{23}{32}$ METER?	NO						0			
$\frac{45}{64}$ METER?	YES							1		
$\frac{91}{128}$ METER?	NO	0	1	0	1	1	0	1	0	= L
$\frac{181}{256}$ METER?	?									

The above diagram shows how the length of a piece of string can be expressed in binary digits. The example is fully explained in the text.

"I won't," is one in a million—i.e. 0.000001, and the probability of his saying, "I will," is 0.999999. A little arithmetic will show that $1/2^{20} = 1/1,048,576 = 0.000001$ very nearly, and some work with seven-figure log tables will show that

$$1/2^{0.0000016} = 0.999999$$

How Much Information in a Piece of String?

The following example is intended as an exercise in thinking in bits. We measure the length (L) of a piece of string as a *binary* fraction. We lay the string alongside a meter rule, starting with the knowledge that it is less than a meter long. We write 0. to show that it is under 1 meter. We now decide, is it over $\frac{1}{2}$ m. long? Yes, it is, and we write 0.1. Is it over $\frac{3}{4}$ m.? No, it is not, and we write 0.10. And so on. We are led into making a sequence of binary decisions, to each of which corresponds one digit of the binary fractional number we are building up. But what is happening? These decision are getting harder every time. The string is slightly elastic and we have to pull it straight to measure it, and in doing so we alter its length. In these circumstances we cannot measure to an accuracy greater than $\pm\frac{1}{2}$ cm.

Very well. Having got as far as the value $L = 0.1011010$, let us stop the measuring process, and express the range of error, 1 cm., in the same binary language. It is 0.000000101 m., which happens to be almost the same as the length L moved six places to the right. The first six decisions we made were all significant; the seventh was doubtful (to say the least) and any further decisions would have been valueless, because L is not such an exact quantity. Therefore, the number of useful binary decisions made was six—conveying six bits of information. Note also that

$$\log_2 \frac{0.1011010}{0.000000101} \quad \text{or} \quad \log_2 \frac{\text{(length)}}{\text{(error range)}} = 6 \text{ approx.}$$

Thus, we seem to have a second way of measuring the amount of information, but in fact it is the same, because we can write

$$-I = \log_2 \frac{\text{error range}}{\text{length}}$$

which is getting rather close to the original version. It is not difficult to believe that if all the lengths from 0 to L are equally probable, the probability (p) of this particular length is (error range/length). Note that if the error range had been zero, implying that the string was measured with perfect accuracy, the measurement would contain an infinite amount of information—and this is not surprising, because it would in general have to be expressed by an infinitely long number. Thus we can infer that all such measurements are limited by their degree of accuracy and can convey only a certain amount of information.

As might be imagined, the quantity *error range* or the mathematical parameter that replaces it can only be determined statistically, after a large number of measurements or trials. Consequently I is difficult to assess accurately but careful use of this term has made possible significant advances in both psychology and communications engineering. E. R. W. F. Crossman reports that psychologists have used it to establish the channel capacity in some five distinct forms of communication within the human body. In one of his examples, in the article entitled "Information Theory in Psychological Measurement" in the *Encyclopaedia of Linguistics, Information and Control* (Pergamon Press, 1969), a chorus master with perfect pitch has been found to transmit 5.5 bits of information when pitching a note, as against 2.3 bits for other subjects. Thus the precision gained by training and practice can actually be measured.

Message Compression
The usefulness of a precise definition of information in communications engineering concerns the problem of message compression in busy channels. The following elegant example was devised by C. E. Shannon. Suppose a message has to be sent in code, using only four letters of the alphabet—A, B, C, D—and that in a typical message $\frac{1}{2}$ the symbols are A's, $\frac{1}{4}$ are B's, $\frac{1}{8}$ are C's, and $\frac{1}{8}$ are D's. For example let the message be

ABBAAADABACCDAAB

and note that it is 16 symbols long. Let us now convert these symbols to 0's and 1's as if we were putting them into a computer, and let us allot the shortest sequence to the commonest symbol by having

$$A = 0$$
$$B = 10$$
$$C = 110$$
$$D = 111$$

the transcribed message reads

0101000011101001101101110010

(The sequence of numbers can, in fact, be converted back into the sequence of letters, without any special markers indicating the beginning and end of each letter representation. The code was carefully chosen to this end.)

An interesting thing happens when we apply a further coding into four symbols, converting the digits two at a time, thus:

$$00 = W$$
$$01 = X$$
$$10 = Y$$
$$11 = Z$$

The stream of symbols now becomes

XXWWZYYXYZXZWY

and this is only 14 symbols long. What originally took 16 letters was first repeated in 28 binary digits and finally said in 14 letters only. This surprising result was achieved by making equal use of the letters W, X, Y, Z, and giving them equal probability of occurrence, whereas the use of A, B, C, D, in the original message was grossly out of balance. This is not an isolated piece of clever sleight of hand but is intended to show how we can make the most efficient use of a costly communication channel, for example to and from a moon rocket.

The same type of coding inefficiency besets ordinary languages. Obviously our 26 letters are not equally used, nor are our commonest words always the shortest and the easiest to pronounce. Would it be worthwhile to tackle the enormous task of radically altering our language, and bulldozing a way to replace the one that we have been brought up with, and really rather like? I think not. Besides, these inefficiencies are very small compared with what happens in computing. For convenience of design, computer "words" are all equal. Usually 24, 36, or 48 bits long. This means that in the 24-bit form the word "one," for example, is expressed in binary notation as 111 100 110 111 001 010 100 011. On the other hand the number 5 is 000 000 000 000 000 000 000 101—a number with rather a lot of spare zeros! Even worse, the information within the set of symbols is rarely expressed at all compactly, and the program governing the operations of the computer is rarely written in the most space- and time-saving way. The reason is very simple: to economize in space, time, and size of computer would cost so much in design and construction, and in programming time, that an apparent economy would turn into a glaring extravagance. For instance it is usually cheaper to buy a second computer than to write programs that make the most economical use of an existing one.

Communication by Behavior

The information gained (or lost) by a human being or any animal can be inferred from its behavior. "This rat has now learned his way through the maze," says the experimental psychologist, "I wonder what sort of distractions will make him forget it?" How does the experimenter know what the rat has learned? Only by observing its behavior. When put at the entrance to the maze, hungry, and stimulated by the smell of food, the rat has run in, reached the first junction, turned the right way, reached the second junction, again made

This rat has learned to distinguish between two patterns and to associate one with food or a reward of some kind. The text discusses how much information the rat itself acquires and how much it communicates to its observer during such experiments.

the right choice, and so on until finding the reward of food waiting at the end. It has done this again and again. If there were three two-way junctions on the route the experimenter could even say that the rat had acquired three bits of information. If after a weekend rest the rat made more mistakes for a while, it would have lost some information; but how much would be rather difficult to measure. Here we have an example of communication between rat and experimenter that was quite incidental as far as the rat was concerned. It only wanted its dinner and did not care at all how little or how much it pleased its keepers. If the rat, after hesitating, chose the right path every time, we should probably say it still had its three bits of information stored in its brain but was having some difficulty retrieving them.

Now here comes another question, subtly different from the previous one. How much information was communicated? Not necessarily three bits. If the experimenter believed beforehand that the rat had a 50–50 chance of learning the maze by this time, exactly one bit was communicated.

Quite apart from incidental communications to the profit of experimenters, animals undoubtedly make purposeful communications to each other that change the behavior of their recipients, and these communications often have an important survival value. The territorial song of birds, courtship displays, alarm signals, roars of defiance—nature is full of them. These are all, in principle, quantifiable. Of particular interest is the waggle dance of bees, because it contains rather a lot of information. It is performed within the hive by a worker, and it conveys both the distance and the direction of a new food supply from which the worker has just returned. It is often danced on the vertical surface of a honeycomb, and a special code involving the position of the sun is used to represent, by a line on a vertical plane, the direction of a horizontal line from the hive to the food. What the dancing bee conveys to us humans, and presumably to its fellow workers, is (1) by its regular figure-of-eight crawling, that it has found a rich new supply of food, or a much needed supply of water; (2) by the direction of the straight part of its track, the direction of the food from the hive; (3) by the length of the straight part of its track, or by the time to make a circuit, which is much the same thing, the distance of the food from the hive; (4) by the duration of the dance, as well as by giving samples to other workers, the value of the nectar or pollen it has found. At a rough estimate, all this adds up to eight or nine bits—quite a long message for a tiny insect to convey all at once.

Animal Memory

It is a very long step from animal behavior to human information retrieval from libraries, and there are not many well-defined intermediate stages, but memory is one of them. In the revolution still boiling in the realm of psychology, many outmoded ideas have been swept away either temporarily or permanently. Consciousness and volition are not considered helpful, for example, because they are presuming a much deeper understanding of mental behavior than we possess. However, whether we can explain it or not, we are bound to believe in memory. Any display of learning, by any animal, requires memory; the animal must have a store containing information, and its behavior must be strongly influenced by the contents of this store.

The best animals for experiments in memory are ourselves, because we can talk. With ourselves as subjects, it is easy to see that we can distinguish between at least two ways of remembering. First there is short-term memory, and this is evidenced by our ability to recall a sequence of numbers at the first go. The length of the sequence is pretty much the same for everyone, about 7 to 9 digits. Actually 12 to 20 items can be remembered for about $\frac{1}{5}$ second, but by the time the first few have been spoken, the others fade away. Some interesting tests can be made which must be connected with how short-term memory works. Ask someone to listen while you list 9 well-assorted digits and to repeat them back. He will do so at a fair speed. Now try again with another set of 9, but ask him to say them backwards. He will be successful, and will produce them at a steady rate but it will be very much slower. You will probably get a distinct impression of numbers chasing each other round and round in your subject's head while he is sorting them into the right order! Many variations of this test can be tried and they all show that it is much easier to get the numbers out of the short-term memory in the order in which they went in.

A few minutes afterwards, both you and your subject will have forgotten what the sequence of numbers was (unless you made a special point of learning it). Having a short-term memory like this is a great convenience, because information pours into our sensory receptors all the time, and much of it, though essential at the time, would be a burdensome nuisance if it stayed more than a few seconds. What a nightmare it would be, for instance, after driving a car for 20 minutes through dense traffic, to remember all the oncoming vehicles, the pedestrians, the traffic signals, and other information that had been vital at the time but was quite useless afterwards.

Long-term memory is quite different, but it also plays a very large part in our lives, and it is remarkably unconfused with short-term memory. Language and speech are good examples, but there are thousands of others. The knowledge that enables us to produce a set of sounds to influence the behavior of our hearer in some way we want, even if it is extremely complex, is something we have been developing all our lifetime. It presupposes a remarkable memory, and an equally remarkable retrieval system.

In our present state of scientific knowledge, hypotheses and theories of animal memory should not be regarded as being anything like the ultimate truth. Their value and purpose is to give a basis for experimentation. The diagram on page 22 illustrates a quite famous one by D. O. Hebb of McGill University, Toronto, which he published in 1948 in his book *The Organization of Behavior*. The idea was that when parts of one brain cell, A, are near enough to excite another cell, B, and repeatedly or persistently take part in firing it (causing it to be active), some change takes place whereby A will in future even more easily excite B. The assembly of nine arrows in the diagram represents nine multiple pathways of cells that are interlinked in this way and that might keep on firing (and

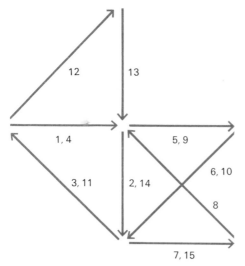

12   13

1, 4   5, 9

3, 11   2, 14   6, 10

8

7, 15

The diagram at left shows an assembly of neural pathways that fire in sequence and thus store information for a longer time than a simple closed circuit (see text).

The diagram below shows how various types of cells in the optic lobe of an octopus are considered to be concerned in the animal's decision-making—in this case, whether to attack or retreat from a certain object. The memory storage cells keep a record of the animal's recent experiences and increase the probability that a certain pathway between a classifying cell and a particular command cell will be activated when the object reappears. When one pathway is active the alternative is inhibited.

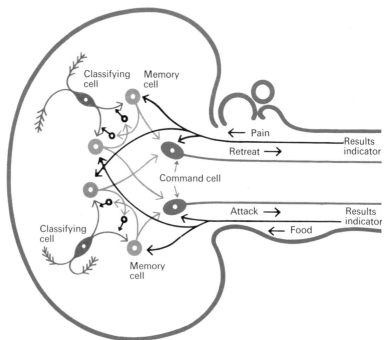

thus storing information) because each cell gets a respite during which it can recover from fatigue. This book has provided a rich source of ideas for researchers all over the world, in psychology, physiology, and engineering, and only in the last year or two has it shown any signs of becoming out of date.

The lower diagram on page 22 shows how an animal's memory cells might be expected to play their part in its decision-making. They must be considered to keep some sort of a statistical record of its experiences, including the present one, and to be especially emphatic about the most recent events.

For a great many purposes, in spite of technological progress, the human brain is still easily the best instrument for information storage and retrieval. Its ability to wander erratically but at great speed through a field of half-relevant facts, and stop at the first sign of finding what it is looking for, is priceless. So is its compactness and portability, its independence of power supplies and environment, and above all its immediate access to receptors bringing input data and to organs of speech and communication. Where the human being has shortcomings, in comparison with machines, is in his ineptness at finding the right card in a bundle, because of his rather naughty way of using heuristic guesswork when he ought to be working tediously and methodically through a huge pile of data.

Store or Memory

In contrast to the elaborate and expensive devices for the entertainment of our sophisticated late-20th-century tastes, it is good to find any innocent survival from the days of our great-grandparents. Talking birds, parrots, cockatoos, minas, budgerigars, any birds that can be taught are still a source of wonder and delight. What makes them memorize the succession of muscular movements for producing these sequences of sounds that we can recognize? Does the bird listen to its own voice and check whether the sounds are identical with some "ghost" sounds it has stored in its brain? It might, but who ever heard of a bird that would stop in mid-sentence and correct itself? Idle speculations like these are little more than

This girl is 20 months old and is learning by trial-and-error methods equivalent to the decision-making processes illustrated on page 22 for the optic lobes of an octopus

a confession that the brain is still very much a mystery.

However, we do have hunches about it, which later generations of neurologists may put on a firmer basis. One is that "remembering by rote" is somehow inferior to learning and remembering by usage. Our multiplication tables—if indeed they are still taught in schools—are tedious enough, especially if we begin by repeating them as if they were just a string of sounds. They are rather easier when we associate other things with them, such as the shapes of the digits, the sequences of odd and even, a special intonation, and so on. When we really want them for a calculation they will come to mind very much more easily if they have been learned in this way. Instead of

A Nigerian tribal leader plays out a story to his people. This is still very common where written records have not yet replaced legends that have remained intact for generations in the memories of storytellers.

having to run right through a section of the table, we shall usually be able to go straight to the place we want, and this surely is a superior way of using our brains. In computer terminology we have *random* or *distributed*, and not merely *sequential* or *serial*, access to our stored multiplication tables.

The accessibility of our stored information is not constant everywhere in the store, however; the more important it is in terms of cost or survival, the more swiftly we can retrieve it, as a general rule. It is now accepted by experts that the human memory is not just a simple store. It is imperfect, but it is selective, retaining those aspects of an experience that seem to matter most. Even more remarkably, it retains things that it did not directly experience. When recalling an encounter with a stranger, we may remember that he spoke with an Irish accent or that the white flower in his lapel was a carnation. Neither of these observations was a simple account of the signals we actually received. We saw an object and, either in rapid succession or simultaneously, deduced (a) that it was attached at a particular place to the stranger's clothing, (b) that it belonged to the color class we call "white," (c) that of the various white objects we might expect to see in that position, it was a flower, and (d) that it was very like some of the carnations we had seen and was therefore a carnation. Sherlock Holmes might sneer, but these simple deductions were enough to put our memory of the event in a different class from the common store such as the jar of sweets in a sweetshop, into which objects are poured and later withdrawn in exactly the same form as they went in.

For these reasons it seems advisable to distinguish between the memories of animals and the stores of computers and other recording devices, avoiding such expressions as "computer memory." All the same, human memory is often used as a simple store of information, naively equivalent to a notebook, or even to a full-sized book, though to a lesser extent than when there was no way of keeping written records. The legends of the remotest Eskimos persisted until quite recently just by being told and retold every winter at the small get-togethers they love so well. The poems of Homer were probably stored for more than a hundred years in the memories of professional storytellers, until the Greek alphabet became available and they were written down. They were so much prized that great efforts were made to keep them uncontaminated by later amendments. Literal memorization of this sort must have helped enormously to keep culture alive until the writing of codices and scrolls was a practical proposition. Folk memory is also interesting in that it corresponds approximately with delay-line storage used in early computers, as we shall see in the next chapter.

This chapter has already encroached on Chapter 2, about Storing Information. We have seen that human memory, if it is to be called a store at all, consists of many inter-connected stores. It performs highly complex operations on all data put into it, and usually we cannot recall in exact detail the same data as went in. Needless to say, the advantages to us, as animals that have to make some decisions in very short times—seconds or fractions of a second—are enormous. However, there are disadvantages too. The loss of exact input data can be very trying and costly, and undoubtedly for this reason our remote ancestors were stimulated to find ways of putting information into other kinds of store. While doing so, they achieved much more than they set out to do. Information was not merely "put in a notebook" for personal use. It was disseminated, handed down from generation to generation, treasured, and sometimes worshipped. Now that we accept that there is a science of information, we have to recognize that this was the very first science to come into being, and the real beginning of technology. In the first part of Chapter 3 these claims will be developed a little further.

2 Storing Information

We have seen that in several ways information is unlike any ordinary commodity. It is valuable, yet even the meanest of us are giving it away all the time and we rarely have to ask for it back, because if we have bothered to remember it we still have it. It is so real, so essential a part of life, that we speak of it in the same way as of sunlight and water. We measure it— rather painstakingly, but then sunlight too is not easy to measure; we send it along "channels"; we let it become contaminated with "noise" and purify it again; and we "store" it.

In its storage, information has remarkable peculiarities, too. When we make a few gallons of home-produced wine we can easily find out how much there is in store and we can also keep a record of what we drink and check from time to time whether there is as much left in the store as there should be. When we store information, however, we seldom measure it, though we often measure how much storage space it occupies. Just as we sample the quality of the wine at intervals we may occasionally verify that the information has not deteriorated

The information store in this carpet loom is the set of punched cards that move around the top of the machine. Each card is read in turn by push rods, the pattern of holes causing corresponding warp threads to be lifted for each throw of the shuttle. This mechanism was invented by Joseph Jacquard in 1801 and punched cards are now an important part of many information-processing systems.

(unlike wine, alas, it cannot improve in store). When we withdraw information from the store, however, it is not consumed, for it can be used again and again. We pay for this by having to find new storage space for every bit of new information that comes our way, unless we are willing to destroy some of the old to make room for it.

The above comments refer to the particular information that we gather and store in special devices of our own contriving, but there are also natural sources and stores of information in our environment. By observing the environment, initially by direct use of the senses and later with the help of instruments, mankind has built up the whole of natural science as we now know it. These observations, which are still going on, are nothing else than reading the information stored in our environment: the positions of stars, the distances between objects, their physical and chemical properties, the growth and behavior of plants and animals, the geological history in rocks, rivers, and seas, the natural history in fossils. To all this we must add the information stored in the more durable artifacts of man—by looking at the pyramids or an electric power supply system we know, more or less, how to build a pyramid or an electric power supply. By looking at a painting we experience something of the feelings of the painter and perhaps of the urge that drove him to paint it. In this chapter, however, we are concerned with the artificial information stores that have been invented in this age of mechanization. Mechanical information stores have two distinguishing features that lift them completely away from comparison with any other store. First, every item in the store is usually different and the job of retrieval involves getting out just the item we want, without considering any of the others. Secondly, there is an enormous number of types and designs of such stores. In order to appreciate the problems of information retrieval from these devices we must first review them in some detail, particularly from the point of view of how information is stored.

The essence of any store is that information can be put in, retained indefinitely without much deterioration, and got out again when required. Some stores have the additional property that they can be erased or otherwise modified and refilled with new information. Putting-in is called *writing*, or sometimes *recording*, and getting-out is called *reading*, or sometimes *playing-back*. If either the writing or the reading is done with electronic or mechanical aids (other than simple hand tools and keyboard devices) the store is considered to be mechanized.

Wheels, Cards, Paper Tape, and Punches

On the above basis, the earliest mechanized store was Joseph Jacquard's invention in 1801 of an important improvement to the mechanical loom. It included cards for controlling which of the warp threads of a piece of weaving were to be lifted for each passage of the shuttle carrying the weft. A pattern of holes was made by hand in each card, and at the appropriate time the card was mechanically read by a set of push rods. Those rods passing through the holes in the card caused the corresponding warp-carrying rods to be lifted and, after the throw of the shuttle, the card was mechanically replaced by the next one. As many as 24,000 hand-punched cards have been used in one weaving operation, a portrait in silk of Jacquard himself, but fewer cards are needed for repetitive patterns. So successful was this invention that it is still in use, for example in carpet-making at Wilton, England (see the photograph on page 28).

The next important store was in a sense the reverse of Jacquard's, for it was mechanically written and visually read. Charles Babbage, between 1822 and 1832, was constructing a Difference Engine for computing mathematical tables. For storage he used columns of wheels, each wheel being capable of resting in any one of 10 positions and so of storing one decimal digit. Babbage's only completed machine, now on show at London's Science Museum, is illustrated on page 32. It has three vertical stores, which in the photograph are set at the numbers 055632, 213740, and 010025. When the lever is pulled once forward and back, the first number is added to the second and the modified second is added to the third. By this means the machine can build up in the third column a series of values of any quadratic function, the simplest being the squares of all the numbers up to 1000. A 14-digit machine with 5 stores was successfully completed a few years afterwards in Sweden. The National Accounting Machine, of American origin, and our modern desk calculators, are the direct descendants of Babbage's invention.

Babbage invented a second calculating machine, which he called an Analytical Engine. He never built enough of this to show its powers, but it is historically of the first importance because it was the first, and for many years the only, general-purpose computer. The modifiable stores in it were of much the same type as in the Difference Engine, but the real innovation was its use of sequences of punched cards, like Jacquard's, for what we should now call *programs* and *numerical data*. The only model of its central computing component, which Babbage called the *Mill*, was made after his death, by his son. Babbage also provided for mechanically printing out the results, and this would have been necessary because they could conceivably have been produced faster than they could be copied by hand. Even here, the inventor had to think very hard, and his solution was for the machine

The forerunner of modern desk calculators, Babbage's 3-ft. high Difference Engine, is shown at left. Babbage developed this computing device between 1822 and 1832. He also spent a great deal of time on a more complex Analytical Engine. This was never completed but in its time represented the first ever general-purpose computer. The Hollerith tabulator shown right is essentially the kind used in the 1890 American census. This 1900 model has a belt-driven card feed and an early type of electric brush sensing device. The bank of "clocks" registers the total number of cards containing holes in particular positions for a batch of cards.

to make a papier-mâché mold in which type would be cast and used to print out the required numbers.

In 1890, sixty years after Babbage's Difference Engine, there was a census in America for which Herman Hollerith, in the U.S. Bureau of the Census, produced and used machines for reading punched cards containing census information and counting those that fell into different classes (see the photograph below). By 1928 a way had been found of using Hollerith machines to calculate, check, and print astronomical tables—positions of the sun, moon, and stars, used for navigating—and these tables were published in the British Nautical Almanack. It was this same need—the production of tables, and the immense labor of doing it with pencil and paper—that had stimulated Babbage to design the Difference Engine 100 years previously. Hollerith punched-card machinery continued for about 25 years to be the best available form of difference engine, though it could never be developed into a general-purpose computer.

A typical Hollerith card, in contrast with one of the rough and clumsy handmade cards of Babbage, has neat rectangular holes in preset positions in 12 rows and 80 columns, and it can store a lot of information in a form suitable for a fast mechanical

reader. Small hand punches are still often used for punching these holes. They have 12 knives, each operated by a key similar to the keys of a typewriter, and by using other keys the card can be slid sideways to any of 80 positions. Machine punches work on the same principle of bringing the card to the right position, and selecting and pushing the right knife. Round holes are punched in paper tape in much the same way — the operator uses a machine with a typewriter keyboard that selects which holes are required in each row and punches a whole row at a time.

Mechanically reading the positions of holes in card or tape is called *hole sensing*, and four ways of doing this are now in use. In the *brush sensing* card reader, which was incorporated in Hollerith machines, each card passes between a metal backing plate or roller and a set of fine wire brushes. These are slightly narrower than the holes and are arranged to coincide with the columns on the card. A timing device connected to the card transport mechanism sends an electronic signal to the control unit as each row of the card passes beneath the brushes. Each hole in the card allows electrical contact between a particular brush and the metal backing plate and a current pulse is sent to the control unit. This registers the exact location of a hole by reference to the column number of the brush and the number of row pulses generated since the card was inserted. Signals from this unit can be fed directly into a computer or used to operate a typewriter or card punch. *Push-rod sensing*, which was first used in Jacquard's loom, was introduced during the 1920s into paper tape machines handling information that did not have to be sorted. This principle is illustrated opposite and is still used today in teleprinters relaying stock exchange quotations and sports results over ordinary telephone lines.

A third method of sensing holes in paper has been used since 1885 in "Monotype" typesetting machines. The paper is much wider, and the holes are larger than in the more familiar paper tape. As the hole reaches the reading head it permits a flow of air, and this opens a valve supplying air to a pneumatic mechanism for selecting the type matrix required and placing

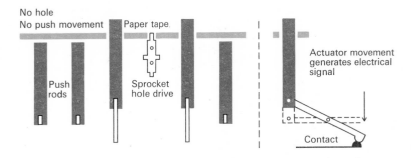

No hole
No push movement

Paper tape

Push rods

Sprocket hole drive

Actuator movement generates electrical signal

Contact

Push-rod hole sensing, diagramed above, is used in stock exchange teleprinters but is not fast enough for use with computers. Punched tape is read into a computer by an optical reader like the one shown on page 49.

it in position. The same sort of paper roll and pneumatic reading was used in a remarkable flourishing of automatic piano playing in the early 1900s. The virtuoso pianists of those times left records of their skill that are even more technically perfect than the most recent phonograph recordings. An example of such a pianola roll is shown on the next page.

The fourth method of sensing, a modern development that employs light and photoelectric cells, will be discussed later in the chapter, where its relevance to modern electronic stores can be better appreciated.

Digital or Analogue?

By about 1940, then, there was available the following choice of mechanical stores and writing and reading devices:

Store: rotating disks with (say) 10 rest positions;
Written: by mechanical rotation of the disks;
Read: by eye or by pressing paper onto type attached to the disks.

Store: holes in cards or paper tape or rolls;
Written: by hand punching, or typewriter operated by hand or electrically;
Read: by brush or rod sensing device, or pneumatically.

The above stores are called *digital* because they contain information corresponding to a number than can be expressed in a finite number of digits. This description becomes clearer when we consider the *analogue* stores that were available in 1940. These by definition contain information that depends on a magnitude, like the reading of a voltmeter or the position

Pneumatic hole sensing, although not used in modern computer devices, has been used since 1885 in "Monotype" typesetting machines. It was also used in pianolas of the early 1900s; the one shown at left is a typical example. The reading head (seen extending each side of the roll) has a row of holes as wide as the paper roll. A pump draws in air through these and, as holes in the roll coincide with them, the inward flow of air causes corresponding notes to be played. So precise was this mechanism that pianists of the day made recordings that exactly reproduced their style.

of any marker along any scale. All recording instruments contain information stores, although at first glance they do not seem to be stores at all. The indicating and recording instruments available at that time included the recording rain gauge, the thermograph, the barograph, the anemograph, and the electroencephalograph. The stores in these devices were written by clockwork and ink and some still are. They were read by eye and only in the last few years have they been read, with analogue-to-digital conversion, directly onto paper tape.

With the above definitions it is not difficult as a rule to put any information store into its right class. Phonograph records and tape recordings of music are obviously analogue, because they store wave records of all audible frequencies and a wide range of amplitudes, which we hear as infinitely variable pitch, loudness, and quality. Speech recordings must be analogue, too, because they are stored in just the same medium. On the other hand, language in any written or printed form is digital. Thus when recorded speech is typed out by an audio-typist the operation is technically a form of analogue-to-digital conversion. Often when natural language is stored in a computer a dictionary is prepared in which every word is given a number and the computer stores sequences of numbers. Digital and analogue technologies have increasingly diverged, and their respective practitioners sometimes seem to be talking different languages. There are, however, *hybrid* computers that employ both analogue and digital components.

Electronic Stores

Already there have been several references to devices, such as magnetic tape recorders and analogue-to-digital converters, that in practice imply the use of electronic techniques. Since 1945, electronics has grown at a stupendous rate and it has permeated the most unexpected places. For example, the desk calculators with their busily churning mechanical barrels are now being ousted by more expensive but perfectly silent ones in which glowing neon numbers wink. Above all, it has made the computer what it is, and the computer—among its many applications—has stimulated numerous studies and experiments in information retrieval. From now on, there will be few paragraphs in this book in which the busy electron does not lurk somewhere between the lines.

The accepted definition of electronics is the study and application of the movement of electrons in a field of force. By this is meant usually a man-made field of force, either an electric field produced by using electric power to maintain potential differences between different parts of a system, or a magnetic field in the neighborhood of permanent magnets or else generated by using electric power in one or more electromagnets. Under these circumstances it is the movement of electrons within a vacuum or a rarefied gas or within a semiconductor that we are interested in. Any movement of electrons in metal wires or sheets is usually incidental.

Scientists really began to understand and learn to control electron movement only during the 1920s. The most important invention at this time was the radio tube or valve. In the valve, electrons are liberated into a space containing gas at a low pressure, from a heated filament called the *cathode*. They will flow from the cathode to a metal plate if the right electric field is maintained between them, i.e. one in which the cathode is negative in relation to the plate, which is called the *anode*. If this field is reversed in direction the electrons will continue to issue from the cathode (because it is heated) but they will no longer flow toward the anode. Thus variation in the electric field between the cathode and anode can be used as a control over the number of electrons crossing the space in a given time, i.e. the total current flowing. This system is called a *diode*. In the *triode*, a third electrode, in the shape of a metal grid, is placed between the cathode and anode, and voltage changes in this cause electrons from the cathode to be either turned back or accelerated toward the anode. Thus small voltage variations in the grid produce large variations in the total current flowing and this is the basis of signal amplification. However, here we are not concerned with how many electrons get to the anode but with the minimum number that must arrive in a particular short time interval to constitute a *pulse*.

It is clear from the definitions in Chapter 1 that an ordinary on-off switch is a one-bit store. The diagram opposite shows how two valves may be used in a circuit as an on-off switch and hence as a one-bit store. It is called a *bistable circuit* and it has two stable states—valve A conducting and valve B off, or valve B conducting and valve A off. The bistable circuit, using valves, was numerous in all computers in the 1950s, and allowed a great leap forward in speed of operation. The first electronic computer, built for military use in Pennsylvania in 1945, contained 18,000 valves. (See also the ACE photograph on page 139).

When valves were superseded by transistors in electronic stores, there was an immediate gain in reliability and compactness, and very much less unwanted heat was generated by the equipment. Nevertheless, bistable circuits continued to be used, and the diagram of a transistor bistable circuit shown opposite is similar to the one using valves.

The modern techniques of making integrated circuits in a chip of semiconducting material produce robust and reliable miniature devices. The one-bit cell shown opposite makes possible the storage of hundreds of bits on a chip only $\frac{1}{4}$ in.

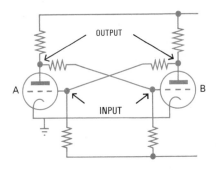
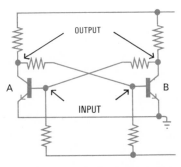

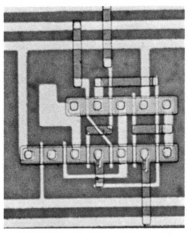

Shown above are typical bistable circuits using triode valves (left) and n-p-n transistors (right). Each circuit changes its state (see text) when a suitable pulse is applied at either of the input points. This causes changes in voltage at the outputs (when one is at the lower voltage the other is at the higher voltage, and vice versa), and either can be used as a reading point. The integrated circuit shown at right is a one-bit cell used in fast-acting stores. It contains 12 MOS transistors (see text), 4 of which form a bistable circuit, and measures only 0.015 in. square.

square. It contains 12 metal-oxide-semiconductor (MOS) field-effect transistors, four of which form a bistable circuit; the remaining transistors are used to set this circuit in either of its two states. This self-contained unit is only 0.015 in. square and is typical of the kind of circuits being used for extremely small, fast-acting stores.

An interesting outcome of the use of valves in computers has been the development of electronic *ring* or *decade counters.* Each decade counter is a multiple valve with 10 cathodes. The valve has 10 different stable states in each of which only one of the cathodes emits current, causing the gas around it to glow brightly. When the valve receives a pulse in the form of a brief voltage change, the cathode that is on is put off and the next in sequence is put on. The cathodes can be arranged in a ring, or be stacked behind one another in the same glass envelope and be made from thin wire—each shaped into the

The desk calculator shown at left is a silent electronic version of the mechanical counters inspired by Babbage's Difference Engine shown on page 32. The numbers show up as shaped cathodes in each of the multiple valves emit electrons, causing the gas around them to glow brightly.

digit corresponding to its position in the firing sequence. When the ninth cathode is put off and the zero cathode put on, a signal passes to an adjacent decade counter producing a "carry." Thus, several counters linked up in a row can be used to register a high number of incoming pulses. Such assemblies are very useful for counting cycles, such as the vibrations of a quartz crystal used as a highly accurate time standard, and they are also the basis of the silent desk calculators mentioned earlier (see the photograph above).

Delay-line Stores

Computers must have rapid automatic means of switching signals from circuit to circuit, and we have seen examples of how this is done by bistables in which electrons flow along wires, across gas-filled spaces, or through semiconductors. There are many other designs of circuit using these principles, and some (if not all) of them can be regarded as stores. Computers also require very large stores, to accept information from the pulses of electron movement and keep it until some other pulse is sent with the object of modifying it, or reading what is there. A million bits of storage is not unusual nowadays, and even the early computers were capable of such a capacity, but expense became the limiting factor. Bistable circuits are not nearly cheap enough, and something easier to make was needed. One method, which has not yet gone out of use, was to use the properties of sound waves.

It is well known that sound waves travel through solids, liquids, or gases, by virtue of the elasticity of the medium. Solids also have a second form of elasticity when in torsion: if a small but sharp twist is given to one end of a long rod, the twist travels rapidly at constant speed right along the rod, to be reflected back from the far end. Both forms of elasticity are used to store many bits of information, with the help of electronics for pulse regeneration, and the device is called a *delay line*. The best materials for delay lines are either mercury, contained in a steel tube up to 5 ft. long and $\frac{1}{2}$ in. diameter, or a thin nickel rod about 1 ft. long and $\frac{1}{10}$ in. diameter.

A sequence of, say, 10 waves, to represent one bit, can be fed into one end of these delay lines, through a transducer, by piezoelectric strain of a quartz crystal in the first case and by magnetostriction in the second. (Piezoelectric strain is the slight mechanical deformation of a crystal when an electric field is applied. Magnetostriction is the deformation of a magnetic material, such as iron or nickel, when a magnetic field is applied.) The diagram below shows the transmission of part of a binary number whose digits are 0110010 along a 5-ft. mercury delay line. A sequence of 10 compressions and rarefactions (carrier waves) generated at transducer A represents the digit 1 if present and 0 if absent. (A completely undisturbed delay line contains a string of 0's, the number depending on the reading equipment used.) Each sequence, of duration 0.67 microsecond, reaches the other end of the line about 1000 microseconds later, but the carrier waves will have

Below: part of a binary number traveling through a mercury delay line (see text). Right: two mercury delay lines. The large one (capacity 1536 bits) has wave reflectors at the bottom, and 5 ft. of mercury between the two transducers. The small, straight one has a capacity of 192 bits.

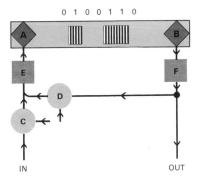

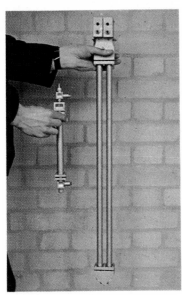

lost some of their regularity. However, each sequence can be read—that is converted back into an electrical pulse—by a device B, exactly like the input transducer A; and then with units F and E it is not difficult to regenerate electronically a perfect sequence of carrier waves and reinsert them at the input end. So the information goes around and around, in one direction with the speed of sound, and back again with the speed of light.

Delay lines were used as medium-sized, rather fast stores in earlier computers, and they had the virtue that any part of the information, even a single bit, could be changed by applying a suitable pulse or nonpulse at the appropriate instant at the input end, using the switch controls C and D in the diagram. They are still the best and cheapest store for some purposes— for instance, to store a message that is being set up with a typewriter keyboard, to display it on a cathode-ray screen, and to permit it to be modified before it is dispatched to a computer or to another store. (See the photograph of a cathode-ray display screen on page 48.)

Magnetic Stores

To store the information that a pulse of electrons has been present this pulse must be made to leave its mark in some form or other. The compression wave running along a delay line is one sort of mark. Magnetic marks, in which each electron pulse changes the magnetization of a strip of magnetic material, are even more important and useful ones.

Tapes, Drums, and Disks. As we may guess, the domestic tape recorder and the tape deck of a computer—so familiar because it happens to be its most photogenic part—are basically one and the same thing. The storage medium in each case is a layer of carefully prepared particles of Fe_2O_3, magnetic iron oxide. The tape is rapidly drawn past a small gap between the pole-pieces of an electromagnet and, whatever difference in current is input to the winding of the electromagnet, a corresponding change in magnetization is recorded on the tape. This can be read back—i.e. reconverted to electrical signals—by drawing the tape past the pole-pieces a second time, having made a suitable modification to the electronic circuit attached to the winding. In design detail, however, the sound recorder and the digital recorder do differ. The acoustic tape has to store a linear continuum of signal strengths, and it is of course an analogue store. The digital tape stores only two alternative directions of magnetization, and for the sake of compactness and, above all, of speed, it has to change its polarity of magnetization in as short a space as possible without a fault.

For the sort of information retrieval to be discussed in this book, we are interested mainly in digital tapes. There are two points of special interest about these. One is the necessity to stop and restart frequently, with minimum loss of time, because usually only certain parts of a tape's information have to be read or written on any particular occasion. This means in practice that it is best to store information in blocks of up to about 20,000 bits, and to introduce a mechanism for counting the blocks rather as if they were pages of a book. Pneumatic capstans are used for driving the tape (no electromagnets can be used, because they could spoil the magnetization of the tape). The other point is the question of errors and the stoppages they might cause. The standard tape in use now is $\frac{1}{2}$ in. wide and can be written in 7 or 9 channel mode, each character being made up of 6 or 8 bits across the width of the tape. The remaining channel is used to make the number of 1's across the tape even or odd (depending on the checking equipment used) and is called the parity channel. The powerful tape-transport mechanism (and the precision with which this has to present the tape to the pole-pieces of the reading and writing heads) and the electronic parity-checking device make a digital magnetic tape unit a costly and demanding piece of equipment. It is suitable for use only in an air-conditioned (temperature- and humidity-controlled) dust-free room, and it has its own built-in air filter and air cooler.

Ignoring any cost of previously preparing the data, magnetic tape is the cheapest storage material we have yet found, except typescript, perhaps. A reel of it may contain over 20 million bits of information, equivalent to half a million words in the

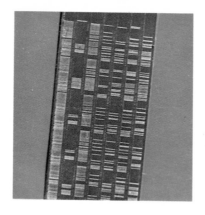

The information encoded on this standard ½-in. magnetic tape has been shown up by applying a "magnetic solution." The marks represent 1's, absence of a mark represents a 0. The parity track is at far left and characters are composed of six bits, one bit taken from each of the remaining six tracks across the width of the tape. The schematic diagram of a magnetic drum at right shows the arrangement of tracks and read/write heads. The exchangeable disk unit shown at far right has six disks and can store a total of 24 million bits.

usual typewriter code. This can be written or read in about 30 minutes. If a particular section has to be found, by counting blocks until it is reached, up to 7 minutes may be needed. This is an unacceptably long time for many purposes, including information retrieval, so other magnetic layer devices (such as drums and disks) have been invented, with a much shorter access time.

Magnetic drums differ from magnetic tapes in that they move smoothly and continuously without stopping. The early magnetic drum was a cylinder about 9 in. in diameter and 12 in. high, rotating at a constant speed of about 2000 rpm around its vertical axis. It was coated with magnetic iron oxide, and the reading and writing were done with a number of magnetic heads equally spaced throughout the height. If, for example, there were 16 heads spaced ¾ in. apart in a frame that could itself be set in 1 of 16 positions, there would be 256 separate tracks of information. If each track contained space for 1024 bits there would be room for over 250,000 bits on the drum. To set one of the heads opposite a given track takes a little time, and to wait for a given point in the track to whirl around to the head takes nearly as long again, with the result that about 20 milliseconds (ms.) are needed to start reading from a drum or writing on it. Some modern drums have a separate head for each track, however, and a very short access time. The most efficient ones can store up to 4 million bits, but this is only one-fifth of the storage capacity of a magnetic tape, and they are much more expensive. Reels of tape are also much more portable and easier and quicker to fix into reading devices than are magnetic drums. Consequently the uses of

Magnetic coating

Tracks

Read/write heads

these two magnetic devices have become complementary rather than competitive. Tapes are used for shelf storage of information for computers, compiler programs, library programs, customer's programs, and data. Drums are used as backing stores to relieve the main stores of a computer from overfilling, and for frequently modified data such as seat reservations.

Magnetic disks are simply a variation on magnetic drums, in which both surfaces of a pile of disks carry the magnetic coating, the disks being sufficiently separated for the reading and writing heads to move between them. They are worth while when an access time of a few tenths of a second can be tolerated, and particularly if an unusually large amount of storage is needed. A unit containing 6 fixed disks can store 400 million bits—enough, for instance, to hold all the information in the card index of a large lending library. Exchangeable disk units, like the one shown above, have only about one-tenth of this capacity.

Core Stores. Magnetic iron and steel are not easy to use as stores for rapid reading and writing of information because they are metals, and therefore good conductors of electricity. Any sudden change in their magnetization produces eddy currents in them that both absorb energy and greatly slow down the magnetization process. In the 1940s the ferrites were developed—a group of compounds that are magnetic, good insulators, hard, durable, and workable into precise shapes. They are made by combining magnetic iron oxide (Fe_2O_3) with oxides of other metals, such as magnesium oxide (MgO), manganese oxide (MnO), and zinc oxide (ZnO), at moderate temperatures. Ferrite cores are made by grinding this fairly soft material to a powder to break up the larger crystal domains, pressing the powder to the requisite shape, and sintering it at about 1200°c. By 1955 ferrite core stores for computers were coming on the market and played a large part in the evolution of what are now known as first-generation computers into second-generation ones.

Each individual ferrite core is a small ring of about $\frac{1}{20}$ in. diameter with a hole of about $\frac{3}{100}$ in. As is well known, a wire carrying a current is surrounded by concentric circles of magnetic lines of force. If a wire threading a ferrite core is given a suitable current, the core becomes magnetized and stays like that. A current in the reverse direction changes the direction of this magnetization. Thus a core has three stable states: unmagnetized (unwritten) and two directions of magnetization (written). A core magnetized in one direction

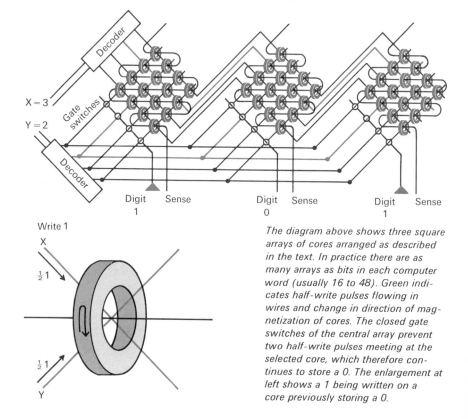

The diagram above shows three square arrays of cores arranged as described in the text. In practice there are as many arrays as bits in each computer word (usually 16 to 48). Green indicates half-write pulses flowing in wires and change in direction of magnetization of cores. The closed gate switches of the central array prevent two half-write pulses meeting at the selected core, which therefore continues to store a 0. The enlargement at left shows a 1 being written on a core previously storing a 0.

can be said to be storing a 1, and one magnetized in the other direction a 0. The unwritten state is not used for storing information.

Reading is done by threading another wire through the cores and sending a current through the write wires of any particular core. If this current causes the direction of magnetization of the core to be reversed, the burst of energy liberated during this change induces a current pulse in the read wire that can be sent to an output terminal or wherever else it is needed. Reading is thus destructive and, once read, a core must be rewritten.

In practice each core is not usually afforded the luxury of its own separate write and read wires. To save space and to simplify the wiring, the cores are positioned at the intersections made by two sets of write wires set at right angles to each other (see the diagram opposite). With such a *square array* a very economical way of magnetizing any particular core exists. This makes use of brief electric pulses that are a little more than half the strength needed to change the magnetization of a core. Suppose the chosen core is in the third X row and second Y row. One *half-write pulse* is sent along the third X wire and another is sent simultaneously along the second Y row wire. As a result the chosen core becomes magnetized (or its magnetization is changed) and all the other cores are unchanged. One read wire threads all the cores diagonally across the array and this detects whether two experimental half-write pulses in the writing wire change the magnetization of the relevant core; if the magnetization changes, the read wire carries a pulse, and the inference is that the core value was 1 (but is now 0).

So far, each array of $n \times n$ cores would need $4n + 2$ wires leading off into other parts of the computer. However, further economy in writing can be achieved by stacking the square arrays in parallel planes and connecting the X wires of each plane in series with the next, and the Y wires of all planes in parallel. To prevent cores in all but the right plane from becoming magnetized, each Y wire has a gate switch, controlled by a digit wire. As the diagram shows, a number is stored by

The display unit shown in use at left is an extremely versatile and convenient device. In this photograph the operator has used the keyboard to set up information in delay lines and has checked it as displayed on the cathode-ray screen. It can now be sent to a computer by pressing another key. The same unit can be used as a terminal for on-line communication with a computer (see Chapter 6). In the optical tape reader shown at right, a narrow beam of light is focused across the width of the moving tape. Holes allow light to penetrate to accurately positioned photocells and the pulses produced are fed into a computer or a print-out device.

putting 0's and 1's at the same XY address in all planes simultaneously. The number of planes thus equals the number of bits per computer word.

As mentioned earlier, when a core storing a 1 is read, it is changed to a 0, and usually a 1 must be rewritten. Thus instead of *access time* we have to consider what is called the *cycle time*. For a high-quality core store this will be 2 or 3 microseconds (μs.), but by abandoning the economies in the two previous paragraphs and reverting to a single array with two separate read and write wires threading each core, cycle times of $\frac{1}{2}$ μs. are possible. The smaller stores with special functions are usually the ones to be given this extra speed. The size of the main core store can be whatever the user requires. It is usually built up in units of 200,000 to 400,000 bits, and computers with four or more units are not uncommon.

Core stores and magnetic drums and disks are called *random access* stores, to distinguish them from *serial access* stores such as magnetic or paper tape. Finding a particular bit of information takes less time in a random access store than it does in a serial access store.

Electrostatic Stores

One other kind of electronic store is very different in principle from those already described. It makes use of the fact that the surface of an insulating material will hold an

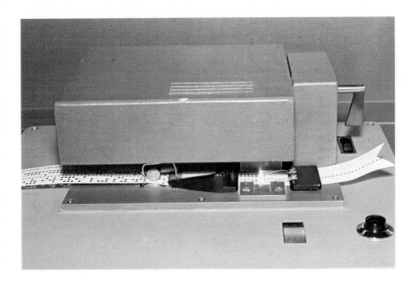

electric charge for a second or two. In the 1950s the possibility of using it in computers was seriously considered, but
now electrostatic storage is used for direct human reading.
If the insulating surface contains one of a number of materials
known as *phosphors*, any charged part of it will glow. The
cathode-ray tube is an outstandingly useful form of such an
electrostatic store. In television sets it displays information
that changes 25 or 30 times per second, but it may be used to
retain any picture for an indefinite time if it is linked to a conventional magnetic or delay-line store from which the information is read and displayed again and again (as shown in
the photograph opposite).

To increase the persistence of the visual display, and decrease the frequency with which it must be refreshed by re-
reading the store, the interior of the visible surface of the
cathode-ray tube is coated with a phosphor that holds for a
second or so the charge given to it by the cathode-ray electrons,
and glows brightly when charged. This is the commonest
example of an electrostatic store. Another form has a phosphor
that glows for many minutes, and has provision for all or part
of the display to be removed by discharging it.

Electronic Readers and Printers

We have come a long way from the punched cards and paper
tape we began with, but even these are now coming under

electronic control of some kind. For example, punched cards and paper tape can be electronically read by illuminating one side of the card or paper tape as it passes in front of a row of miniature photoelectric cells. The photocurrents produced when light penetrates the holes are transmitted as electronic pulses. Another use of photoelectric cells is in *mark-sensing*: a storeman will record a delivery, for example, by marking black pencil marks in the appropriate positions on an especially printed card. A batch of such cards can afterwards be read with equipment in which the photoelectric cells detect reflected light, and the information passed directly into a computer.

Electronic equipment is also used in very fast punching of paper tape—for example, in reading the output of a computer; by this means much of the inertia of purely mechanical equipment can be avoided. Much ingenuity has gone into designs for stopping the tape at the place where the knives have to punch holes, and then restarting it. In one form, the sprocket drive is lifted out of position by a very strong helical spring. The knives are actuated by electromagnets, but these cannot release energy in a form concentrated enough to do a really

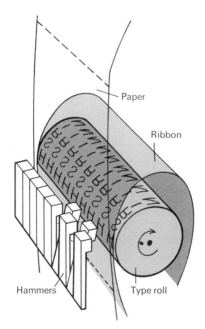

Paper

Ribbon

Hammers   Type roll

For efficient use of computers, associated reading-in and printing-out devices must operate at high speed. The line printer (whose speed is compared with other peripheral devices and certain types of computer stores in the table opposite) is used for rapid conversion of electronic signals (from tape or computer) into humanly readable form. The signals operate a row of hammers and—as shown in the diagram—each hammer is opposite one ring of alphanumeric characters on the type roll. As each selected character comes around, the appropriate hammer is activated and a whole line is typed during one revolution of the roll.

Capacities and Access Times

Store	Typical capacity	Access time
Delay line	40 characters	average 200μs
Core store	10,000 to 50,000 characters	cycle time 0.3 to 3μs
Bistable circuit	1 bit	5ns to 1μs
Magnetic tape	2400 ft. storing 800 characters/inch i.e. 20,000,000 characters	average 3 minutes for a block
Magnetic card	600 characters	400 ms
Magnet drum with fixed heads	2,000,000 characters	average 10 ms
Disk file with moving heads	50,000,000 characters	average 220 ms

Speeds of Reading and Writing Devices

Tape- and card-operated typewriters	10-50 characters/sec.
Tape and card readers, generating electronic signals	up to 1000 characters/sec.
Strip (or line) printers, 132 characters/line	up to 15 lines/sec.
Magnetic tape, reading or writing head	100,000 characters/sec.

1 second = 1000 milliseconds (ms) = 1,000,000 microseconds (μs) = 1,000,000,000 nanoseconds (ns).

fast job of punching, so their function is merely to trigger off the main energy stored in powerful steel leaf springs, and to reset the springs after use.

The need for rapid conversion of information on magnetic tape or in a computer store into humanly readable form has led to the development of the strip or line printer (see the diagram opposite). This uses a roller rotating at up to 1000 rps, with 64 (or more) rings of type mounted on the cylinder, each ring having the full set of alphanumeric characters. The paper is held just clear of the roller, with 64 light metal pads behind it, and an electric pulse causes each pad to press onto the paper and the paper onto the type. The information signals are used to operate each pad just as the required character comes round. In this way one whole line of typing is done during one revolution of the roller and the paper is then moved on ready for the next line of type.

Speeds and Speed Matching

An individual device rarely operates quite independently of any other. Nearly always, one device is reading information

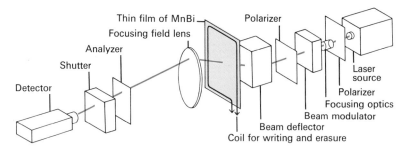

Thin film of MnBi
Focusing field lens
Analyzer
Shutter
Detector

Polarizer

Laser
source
Polarizer
Focusing optics
Beam modulator
Beam deflector
Coil for writing and erasure

The diagram and photograph show how a laser and a manganese-bismuth film can be used to store information. For writing, high-intensity laser pulses are focused on a selected point of the film, heating it momentarily above 360°C (see text). A suitable magnetic field is produced by a current in the coil and as the point cools it becomes magnetized in a corresponding direction. For reading (as above), low-power laser pulses are polarized and focused on a selected point. The transmitted beam is monitored to detect which way the magnetization has rotated the plane of polarization (one way representing a 1, the other a 0).

and converting it into electrical signals, and another is re-converting the signals into a different form of stored information. *Device* in this context means any of the stores, readers, writers, or printers that we have been considering in this chapter, together of course with any kind of electronic computer. The devices that receive signals from a computer or send signals to it are called its *peripherals*. In general, the peripherals of a computer are chosen to work at great speed, and to leave the computer as free as possible to get on with its computing. Similarly any two devices for use in communication with each other should be matched in speed, particularly if one of them is expensive. At the slow end of all this is the

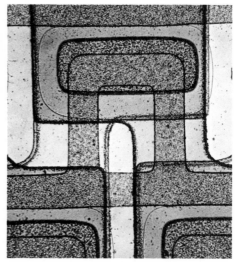

Above: part of an experimental super-conducting memory plane containing over 13,000 one-bit cells per square inch. Right: the tin loop of one of these cells is visible in the center of this photomicrograph (enlarged 180 diameters). Under- and over-lying lead sections are also visible.

human reader or keypuncher, and he has to be matched with such equipment as the printed book, the typewriter, or the cathode-ray tube display. He (or she) is reckoned as a rather expensive, slow, but extremely versatile device, to be used if possible in tasks where computing and access to complicated data goes along in parallel with plain data processing.

Many considerations—such as cost, maintenance, reliability, and delivery date—go into the choice of hardware for a system, but speeds and speed matching are the most important among them. A general idea of the speeds that must be considered when planning any computer system is shown in the list on page 51.

A Look into the Future

Without at the moment considering what use would be found for them, what new kinds of stores could we expect the ingenuity of man to produce? Nothing seems likely to supersede the electronic or electromagnetic signals, and therefore all the more advanced stores are likely to be electronically written and read. Both electronic and electromagnetic motions are limited by the speed of light, approximately 3×10^{10} cm/sec in vacuo. A light beam could conceivably carry pulses separated by a distance of 1 micron (10^{-4} cm.), this being about twice the wavelength of light. Thus in each 1 cm. of light tube, 10^4 bits could be stored, and presumably each bit could be read or written in $1/3 \times 10^{10} \times 10^4$ sec. or $3\frac{1}{3}$ millionths of a nanosecond (ns.).

Light in its coherent, concentrated form as produced by lasers is already being developed for writing and reading very closely packed information. The storage medium is a thin film of a ferromagnetic material such as europium oxide, or manganese-bismuth. A laser pulse focused on a small area of manganese-bismuth, for instance, will in 1 μs. raise its temperature above the Curie point, 360°C. Any magnetic alignment in the material is destroyed at these temperatures, but while cooling once more below the Curie point—a process, that again takes about 1 μs.—the treated area will take up the alignment of whatever magnetic field is in the vicinity (i.e. that induced by a coil). The film can be read by scanning it with a much weaker, polarized beam from the same laser. The magnetized area changes the direction of polarization of the laser and the transmitted beam is passed through a polarizing-glass analyzer onto a photoelectric cell (see the photograph and diagram on page 52).

A third kind of store, which has been the subject of experiments for the last 10 years, also seems to be nearing the prototype stage. This is the cryoelectric store, which has to be kept in liquid helium at 3.5°K (−269.5°C), and it depends on the superconductivity of two particular metals at this extremely low temperature. Lead is indestructibly superconductive at 3.5°K—that is, a wire or film of it can carry a large current without showing any resistance at all. Tin is likewise superconductive, but only if it is in zero or weak magnetic fields. A small piece of tin film is sandwiched between two small lead films, which are joined at one edge to make a loop. When the lead loop is given a current, the magnetic field it produces destroys the superconductivity of the tin, giving it a non-zero resistance. The effect is like that of an extremely fast-acting switch, which can be used to store one bit of information. Cryoelectric stores based on this principle are being planned to hold 100 million bits in the quite small volume of 125 cc. (see the photographs on page 53). They will be random access stores with a cycle time of 4 μs. and compared with large core stores will be relatively cheap.

The cryoelectric store is only one of several integrated storage devices that, if they can be made cheaply and reliably, will offer increased speed through miniaturization, and avoid the difficult threading process used for core stores. One alternative is the monolithic ferrite store, in which three layers of ferrite are sintered together and contain two sets of conducting wires at right angles to each other. Another idea is to use permalloy films. Permalloy is a nickel-iron alloy that does not suffer from sluggishness due to eddy currents if it is formed in thin enough sheets—less than about 0.00025 in. (0.00062 cm.). Films of it can be made that are easy to magnetize in one direction but hard to magnetize at right angles to this direction. This is a design advantage, and permalloy flat thin-film stores are already in production, with cycle times of less than 500 ns. (0.5 μs.). Prototypes of even faster stores have been built, in which the permalloy is electroplated on beryllium-copper wires, threaded through loops in other wires.

Finally, significant advances are to be expected in a store that has already been mentioned, for reading by eye: the display. It would be difficult to decide at the present time whether the major improvements will use the cathode-ray tube (several developments of which are being tried out) or some other kind of device—such as various assemblies of neon tubes or the glowing digits already used in desk calculators. The importance of the display is that it can be used to put a human being into direct communication with a computer without wasting any of the computer's speed. We shall see, later on, how displays can be used in conjunction with big computer stores for library information retrieval.

3 The Library as a System

The greatest and most vital store we have is the world's store of information in books, periodicals, documents, recordings, inscriptions, photographs, paintings, drawings, and sculpture. The first four occur mainly in a multitude of identical copies, most of which, when they are not in warehouses or shops, are to be found in libraries of one sort or another. The last five, together with archaeological collections, are to be seen in galleries, museums, and even in the open air along with architecture and civil engineering works.

Like any other store of information, the world's literature store has a range of write and read times, and access times. These times, and the economic costs that go with them, are what information retrieval is about. Principally it is concerned with access time and cost, and there has been a tendency to ignore or leave to scholars the question of language, reading, and writing. However, the study of language, at any rate, has recently undergone what must be its greatest expansion ever; mathematicians have entered the field, and linguistics is now

A typical lending library at work. Users browse through likely books or search the Classified Catalog for specific titles. These activities are familiar to us all, but they reflect only a part of the library's work, which includes keeping scientists and other specialists up to date in their own particular fields. This and later chapters discuss how library services can be facilitated and expanded with the help of computers and mechanical aids.

a science rather than an art. The fact that "languages" are needed in computer programming, and in talking and writing about computer programs, is one but not the only cause of this change of emphasis.

Writing

Having made this point, we shall follow the trend and consider mainly the access aspects of information retrieval; but first a brief look should be taken at its most neglected sides, those of human writing and reading. As Dr. David Diringer states: "Writing is at one time the most universal and the most elusive of things. It has escaped formal study in most universities, yet every scholarly discipline touches upon it at some point, and often in matters of considerable importance. . . . The possibilities inherent in oral transmission are far wider than was conceived a century or two ago, but, in comparison with the worlds opened up by the use of writing, they are bounded by fixed and absolute limits. . . . We can with justice, therefore, speak of writing as so uniquely useful and powerful a craft that to call it an 'instrument' is implicitly to understate. At a time when the distinction between subjective and objective was less clear-cut than it is today, it seemed to most men a magic power: a connotation which continued to cling to it even in the West until comparatively recent times."

In his books *Writing* (Thames and Hudson, 1962) and *The Hand Produced Book* (Hutchinson, 1953), Diringer divides all ancient writing into *epigraphy* which is inscription on stone and hard materials for all to see whether they like it or not and *paleography* on paper and soft materials for one or more people to read and re-read as they wish. We are more concerned about the successors to paleography, because speeds of writing, reading, and access, matter so much to us. Paradoxically, however, it is largely through studies of epigraphy, where speed is unimportant, that evidence of the most brilliant of all linguistic inventions, phonetic alphabetic writing, is being uncovered.

For an intelligent savage, who wants to record some important information but who has no previous experience of

this problem, the natural thing to do is to make marks in sand
or on stone perhaps. It is natural, also, that these marks should
look like the objects they represent. After being copied and used
in other contexts, in the course of time the marks may become
standardized and conventionalized, and their power will be
improved by the addition of signs representing actions—
a mouth for speaking, a pair of jaws for eating, and so on.
Developments of this sort have happened often, probably quite
spontaneously, in most parts of the world where primitive
man has settled. Numerous sets of such *pictographs* are known,
as are many more advanced, *ideographic* scripts. These are
made up of symbols that can represent not only the thing they
show, but also ideas associated with that thing. Notable
examples are Egyptian writing, most forms of cuneiform, the
scripts of pre-Columbian America, the Indus Valley and other
places. Modern Chinese is an ideographic script and there
are still local pockets of indigenous picture writing in every
continent except Europe.

We need be concerned with only two properties of this kind
of writing. One is that archaic inscriptions can be deciphered
without having the slightest idea of the speech sounds that were
used to describe the objects and actions represented—that
is, if they can be deciphered at all. The other is that the number
of distinct characters is always large: in Chinese, at one time,
there was a list of 44,449. Thus there is always a good way of
deciding whether a newly discovered specimen is ideographic
or phonetic, for the latter will rarely have more than 100 signs.

It must be extremely difficult to learn to read and write any
rich ideographic script. Quite apart from the sheer number of
signs, it is difficult to arrange them in an easily remembered
order for learning or reference, such as the alphabetical order
of a dictionary. No doubt for every long-enduring ideographic
script, and some of them lasted for thousands of years, there
were orderings and mnemonics, but they would be intricate
and far from comprehensive. Likewise it is not surprising that
ideographic writing has never succeeded in developing into
a script that can be easily remembered, and therefore quickly
written and read.

Left: part of the Babylonian Sun-god Tablet (c. 870 B.C.). The cuneiform writing here consisted of 600 or 700 symbols, of which half were phonetic and half ideographic. Cuneiform ("wedge-shaped") writing was derived from Sumerian picture writing at the end of the 4th millennium B.C. It reads from left to right. Above: part of the Moabite Stele (c. 850 B.C.). Moabite script used essentially the same alphabet as Early Hebrew and Phoenician, which originated from the Canaanites around 3000 B.C. It reads from right to left.

Phonetic Writing

To represent objects in writing with symbols for their spoken names, instead of pictures of them, has several advantages. First, the spoken words for actions, emotions, and attributes can also be straightforwardly represented. Second, the list of symbols for speech sounds can be quite short, even if there is a separate symbol for each syllable. A number of phonetic or partly phonetic scripts were invented that were syllabic, and they survived for many centuries. One of the earliest of these was discovered at the ancient Phoenician site of Byblos in 1929, and it has been dated between 1800 and 1400 B.C. There were others in Cyprus and Persia, the latter using cuneiform symbols.

The alphabet was an even more original advance, and Dr. Diringer thinks it may even be the work of one man, probably in about 1100 B.C. on the coastal plain of Syria, at the center of

The Greeks adopted the Phoenician alphabet in the 10th or 9th century B.C. They originally wrote it from right to left but after 500 B.C. they wrote from left to right. The above example is in the 6th-century-B.C. boustrophedon *style (from left to right and then right to left) and comes from the island of Thera, where an earlier form may have been the prototype for all Western alphabets. Right: Irish semiuncial book-hand of the Book of Kells (about A.D. 800), regarded by some scholars as the most beautiful book in the world.*

the main trading routes of those times. He says "It is the kind of sudden intuitive perception which single men like Newton have more than once accomplished, even when others did the elaborating and perfecting."

By representing fractions of the syllables of speech, the letters of the alphabet form a very neat device for storing verbal information. There are only 22–32 of them, depending on the language and mode of use, and they can be arranged in an order that can be easily memorized. They could be improved, as George Bernard Shaw and many others have pointed out, but they are far better than any radically different alternative. Their very imprecision can be an advantage, because it enables them to be much fewer in number than, for instance, the 80 symbols of the phonetician, and because it helps to smooth over local differences of speech.

The development of books and literature is described by

Dr. David Diringer in *The Hand Produced Book*. There were libraries in Syria, Mesopotamia, and Egypt before 2000 B.C. in which the books were of clay tablets. The earliest surviving literary catalog is Sumerian of about 2000 B.C., and at that time there must have been a "vast, varied, and highly developed literature, consisting of myths, hymns, prayers and epic tables, proverbs and aphorisms, lamentations and love songs." In the next millenium there were also plenty of records and documents about law, administration, trade and religion. Because both language and writing were changing continually, there were dictionaries, syllabaries and grammars. It was a tradition then, as now, that young people should learn to read and write, and try to make a career in the professions.

Books changed their medium to papyrus, leather, and parchment, but more ephemeral documents were written on bark, waxed wood, palm leaves and other leaves. The first truly historical writing, according to Harry Elmer Barnes' *A History of Historical Writing* (Dover, 1962) was the Hebrew Old Testament whose earliest known source was written about 900 B.C. When at last the Greeks entered the story, they started apparently with a Semitic alphabetic script and "improved it to such an extent that it has remained for 3000 years, with only slight modifications, an unexampled vehicle of expression and communication for men of the most diverse nationalities and tongues." We owe much to the Greeks for this outstanding development, and still more, of course, for the way they used it.

Human Speeds in Communication

Because they are so familiar, little need be said about the speeds of modern writing and reading. They vary quite a lot with the occasion, but a typical speed of composition, not copying, might be 20 words a minute. This is rather slow in comparison with speech, which sometimes attains 200 words a minute, and this is also about the maximum speed at which verbal information can be comprehended. Reading speeds are more usually in the range 120-150 words a minute. Shorthand can be written by experts at 200 words a minute, but this is when they are copying, not generating new information.

For copy-typing, and transcribing shorthand, 50 words a minute is reasonable. The speed of audio typing, from speech recorded on magnetic tape, is similar. On the whole, the methods we have had for the last 100 years are adequate for most purposes. The most irksome chore is the stenographer's job of transcribing shorthand. First steps to relieve it are already being taken. Operators at conferences, in law courts, and debates make use of shorthand typing machines, depressing 1 to 8 keys simultaneously to produce a row of shorthand symbols as a separate line of type. At the National Physical Laboratory, in the United Kingdom, such machines have been modified to generate signals that a computer (immediately if necessary) converts to an output that a line printer or typewriter prints out in humanly readable form.

Once their conversation or dissertation is on record, those responsible can forget it provided the records can be found again when wanted. Speed of finding can easily be less than speed of reading, but care and skill must always attend the important task of storing the written word.

What is a Library?

Any collection of books and periodicals is a library, this term being derived from the latin "liber" meaning "book" and "inner bark of a tree." A collection of films, photographs, phonograph records, magnetic tapes, or computer programs is also a library, but this diversity is of little consequence, because it will turn out that almost everything that can be written about book and document retrieval is equally true of all the other kinds of library.

All libraries grow most of the time, introducing much work for the librarians, but the immediate and obvious weakness of the standard definition is that it is incomplete and leaves out a most important distinction. A library is a collection of books and a list of their addresses. The word "address" has grown in significance in recent years, because electronic engineers and computer programmers find it so useful. For instance, the following sequence of instructions E 3000; SET 29; X; = E 2888; to one sort of computer means "Fetch the

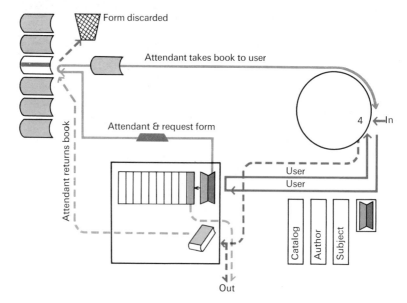

Form discarded

Attendant takes book to user

Attendant & request form

Attendant returns book

4 ←In

User
User

Catalog
Author
Subject

Out

The reading room of the Victoria and Albert Museum Library, London, is shown in use above. The problems and advantages of such a system, in which all the books are guarded, are fully discussed in the text.

number stored at address E 3000, multiply it by 29, and store the result at address E 2888." An address is still the same thing as it ever was: the position in a store, a town, or the universe where a required object will be found.

Any book in its time has many addresses. Its home address is usually a position among other books in the library building, which librarians quaintly call its "shelf number." When it is in use it is not at home, and the librarian has to know its temporary address. How he does this is subject to variation, and it depends on the type of library, but he will almost certainly have a collection of forms, one for each book not on the shelves, giving its temporary address. He might also have a dummy book, a sheet of cardboard, in the home address, containing the same information.

"Most Libraries are a Set of Interlocking Subsystems"

"System" is an *in*-word but it now has a more clearcut connotation than the rather woolly definition in the dictionaries. A system is any organization for the movement of material or information. Examples are hardly necessary, for the most of the organizations of man and nature can be treated as systems, and have to be so treated when they need to be examined closely. Most libraries are not merely a system in which books, librarians, and users all play a part, but they are also a set of interlocking subsystems. Consider first a non-growing library and reading room, no books ever being allowed to leave or enter the library area. The Library of Congress or the British Museum would be such a system if no new acquisitions were made and for a short time, such as a single day, this kind of system could be used as a model for each of these great libraries.

The diagram opposite serves as an elementary description of such a system. It describes the procedure at the Victoria and Albert Museum in London, which contains 300,000 books about Fine and Applied Art. A user enters, chooses a table to work at (all the chairs are numbered) and fills in a form, with a carbon copy, requesting a book and hands it to a librarian. An attendant fetches the book, putting the top copy in its place on the shelf. In this way he can easily find that a book is occupied and locate it accurately within the library. The librarian stores the carbon copy in alphabetical order of the user's name.

The main reading room of the Library of Congress in Washington is shown right. The library is used by congressmen as well as the general public, and over the period of a single day it operates like the nongrowing library shown opposite. The classification system now in use was organized by Dr. Herbert Putnam, and is discussed in more detail in Chapter 4.

When he has finished reading the user returns the book to the librarian's desk and receives the carbon copy as a reference for the press mark (the local vernacular for the shelf address of the book and the most important number) should he want the same book again. The attendant then collects the book, replaces it on the shelf and throws the top copy away.

That is the system, or at least part of it. Suppose the user does not know the shelf address of the book. If he knows the author's name, and the approximate title, he can look up the address in the "author index" which is usually one or more racks of drawers containing cards arranged in alphabetical order of authors' names. If, however, he knows the exact title of the book, he might conceivably find there is another set of drawers with cards arranged in alphabetical order of title, but this is unusual except in small specialist libraries. If he is even vaguer about the book but knows it exists, he has to summon all the scraps of knowledge that he has about it, and look in bibliographies or in the classified list of books in the library. The latter is yet another set of drawers, together with a book or books describing the classification system.

A classification system consists of a set of numbers, or sometimes letters and numbers, arranged in numerical order. To each number there corresponds a different subject, and the vague-minded user must at least know something about the subject matter of the book for which he is looking. He therefore finds the appropriate number or numbers for his subject (in a book describing the classification system) and then looks alongside this number in the Classified Catalog (usually cards in drawers, or loose leaf booklets). The Classification Catalog contains the classification number, title and author of every book in the library, arranged in order of classification number.

There are two other important uses of a classification system. The first is that it will, with certain restrictions and imperfections, produce a definite order for any set of books. Thus it is very often used to determine the shelf order, i.e. the *shelf addresses*, of a library. (Often but not always: the National Lending Library of the United Kingdom, which is essentially a mail-order library, has a shelf order which is primarily determined by the date the library actually receives each new book.) The second important use of classification systems is for browsing. If the shelf order of the books is that of a classification system, the user by looking along the shelf will see a number of books that are related to the one he has in mind. Even if this is not possible, he can browse through the card drawers of the Classified Catalog.

Classification evidently affects a large part of the library system, but that is not all. We shall see in the next chapter that it is much more than just a device for finding books and other objects. It is an essential outcome of the way people think, and, for some specialists, it is almost a way of life.

The diagram we have been discussing represents a fairly simple system in which all books are guarded. It would be even simpler if the user merely had to find his book on the shelf, and leave it on his desk when he had finished. Experience shows, however, that books are lost with such a system, and the addresses of books still physically within the library are also lost. They move to an incorrect address on the shelves; and when a user reports a book as missing from the shelves the librarian has to search all the desks, and possibly all the shelves, to find it.

Another sort of library, familiar to everyone, is the lending library. A flow diagram of a typical one is shown on page 68. When on the shelf, every book has an identifier, a small card tucked inside a flap containing the author's name, the book's title, and classification number and (by implication) its shelf address. Every user has a stock of cards or tickets containing *his* identifier, which may be merely a number referring to a list of users possessed by the library or his full name and address. The book and personal identifiers are stored together in a tray in the order the librarian receives them, and then divided into several trays, one for each main section of the library's classification system. A simple overdue reminder system can then be operated, and this is an example of a sub-system.

An alternative system, based on the use of microfilm to record issuing details, provides the librarian with a more

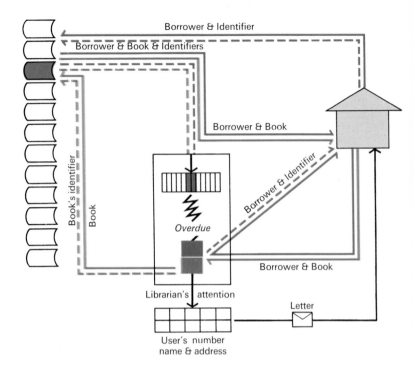

Borrower & Identifier

Borrower & Book & Identifiers

Borrower & Book

Book's identifier

Book

Overdue

Borrower & Identifier

Borrower & Book

Librarian's attention

Letter

User's number
name & address

The lending library flow diagram shown above features the conventional flap-and-ticket system. This and the more recent use of microfilm for recording book details are fully described in the text.

compact method of circulation control. As each book is issued the flyleaf (containing the book's accession number and sometimes the author and title) is photographed together with the borrower's card (containing his name and address) and a date card. The numbered date cards are issued in sequence and stamped before the library opens with the return date—usually three weeks ahead. The borrower takes the date card home inside his book. As the books issued on that day are returned their date cards are filed in numerical order. Any overdue books show up as gaps in this sequence and the librarian only has to look at the microfilm to find the book's identification number and the borrower's name. The 16 mm. film is stored in 100 ft. reels each of which contains details of 5000 books. There is of course a hiatus in the librarian's knowledge of the address of any book on loan. If he was compelled to recover quickly a book that was not on the shelves, he would have to

The photographs above show the mechanized transport system in use at the National Lending Library in Yorkshire, England. At left a library assistant loads the requested books onto a moving tray, which will carry them directly to the dispatch department shown at right. For incoming books the tray can be automatically unloaded at any number of places.

search the entire loan tray or microfilm reels for its identifier, and it might be so costly in his time that it would be cheaper to buy another copy of the book.

So far, the librarian has not been shown in his true light. If he seems to be a mere store keeper, that is because we have paid no attention to the special skill of the reference librarian, who is an authority in a special field. He knows who has written what in this field, where it is published, and the meaning of any special vocabulary used. Another restriction is that we have been imagining libraries with a fixed stock of books. All libraries with which we are concerned have a growing stock, and this is where much of the librarian's time is spent. Quite apart from choosing and acquiring new books, the librarian must introduce (accession) each new book into the system. Nearly all libraries offer various services to their users in addition to the obvious ones of providing books and knowing their addresses, and every additional service makes the task of accessioning more arduous. This is one of the points at which automation can be of help, though libraries are already doing a great deal to lighten this work by cooperating with each other.

The diagram on page 73 shows the Machine Aided Technical Processing System (MATPS) in operation at Yale University Library. The system is designed to monitor and facilitate the issue of books from the time they are requested until they are ready for dispatch. Notice the uses it makes of a computer to keep records of funds, requesters and dealers, changes of addresses of books, and to produce regular lists of books in process.

Services

What are these extra library services, leaving out the scholarly one of giving advice and general assistance to readers? In the first place libraries publish accession lists of new books available as well as regular bibliographies. These must be kept up to date by short sequences of supplements that are frequently merged with the main body to produce "cumulations." Bibliographies are nothing more than lists of books, but what a task their preparation becomes when it is governed by a determined effort to have available any list of books that may be required in the foreseeable future! There must be about 100 million books in existence, counting each title once only. If on average each title, with its author and publisher, were to appear in only 5 bibliographic lists, the resulting 1000 million lines of print would fill 10,000 volumes the size of a volume of the Encylopaedia Britannica. Many cumulative bibliographies are produced by the national institutions such as the Library of Congress and the British National Bibliography (B.N.B.) in cooperation with the British Museum, and these are extensively used in most of the world's libraries. They are used in selecting books for purchase, and in helping enquirers who want to search the literature for special purposes. The B.N.B. is really a set of bibliographies, listing once and often more than once every book deposited since 1950 at the British Museum as publishers are obliged to do according to the Copyright laws.

Information Centers

When a library provides periodicals its services may assume an entirely new character, that of the *information center*. Barbara Kyle, in *Teach Yourself Librarianship* (E.U.P., 1964) gives as an example the library of the Royal Institute of International Affairs in London. It is run primarily for the members of the institute, but if it were a public institution, capable of handling enquiries from other libraries, it would be more typical of many information centers now coming into being. It receives 535 periodicals in 16 languages, as well as daily newspapers. "Every day the papers must be read—and not only English papers. Reports from journalists, communiqués from statesmen and government officials, press releases outlining government policies and summarizing texts of treaties, all these and much more are cut, mounted, classified and filed. The collection of press cuttings (by 1964) numbered more than five million, and within five minutes of entering the door a member can have on his desk an orderly anthology of information on, for example, the Cuban crisis. . . . Each week in the library 163 periodicals in five languages are read and their relevant contents indexed. Here again, within five minutes a reader may receive on his desk articles giving American, French and Commonwealth views on Britain's possible entry into the European Common Market."

An organization that pays particular attention to Information Centers is the Batelle Memorial Institute at Columbus, Ohio. In 1968 it had 14 specialist information centers in being, including one for supplying environmental information on request to all residents in the Columbus area. David M. Liston Jr. of its Research Division in an article entitled *Information Systems* (1966) commented that two general types of information centers were emerging: discipline-oriented information centers and mission-oriented information centers. The discipline-oriented centers were expected to grow very large and to divide the coverage of information along disciplinary lines. Typical discipline divisions might be Medicine, Chemistry, Physics, Engineering, Sociology, Philosophy. For example, there were already proposals for an Engineering Information Center resulting from cooperative efforts of the Engineering Index, the Engineering Societies Library, the Engineers Joint Council, and the member societies of the Engineers Joint Council.

David Liston suggested as examples of mission-oriented centers a Surgical Instruments Information Center, a Packaging Information Center, a Fasteners Information Center, and a Protective Coatings Information Center. He pointed out that the discipline-oriented center may serve as a wholesaler of information to the mission-oriented center. In turn, the mission-oriented center may serve as a retailer of information to individual corporations or other organizations as well as to individual scientists and engineers. For example a Protective Coatings Information Center certainly would draw some of its information from the coverages of both an Engineering Information Center and a Chemistry Information Center and retail it to a wide variety of manufacturers.

Libraries and the Scientist

The work of the Batelle Memorial Institute is a reminder that by far the largest class of individuals in need of up-to-date information are the scientists, who constantly run the risk of wasting their time, equipment, and the funds supporting them, or wasting their firms' opportunities, through neglecting to take into account the knowledge gained and published by other members of their fraternity. In an article on "Scientific Documentation" in the *Encyclopaedia of Linguistics, Information and Control* (Pergamon, 1969) H. East and J. Martyn stated: "Originally the working scientist would cover his day-to-day needs for current awareness information by subscribing to the few journals that he felt he needed to see on a regular basis. Nowadays the more common practice is for the scientist to instruct his library to acquire and circulate to him such journals as he feels he needs to see, and such others as they may acquire and judge worthy of his attention. Since this approach nowadays is liable to flood the scientist with an embarassingly large number of titles, attempts have been made to relieve him of the necessity of scanning this large number of journals. This is often done by the publication, either by a commercial organization or a learned society, or on a smaller scale by the scientist's librarian, of lists of titles of papers to be found in selected current journals" (see Chapter 5).

Librarians recognize at least some of the needs, perhaps better than many of the scientists themselves, but any one

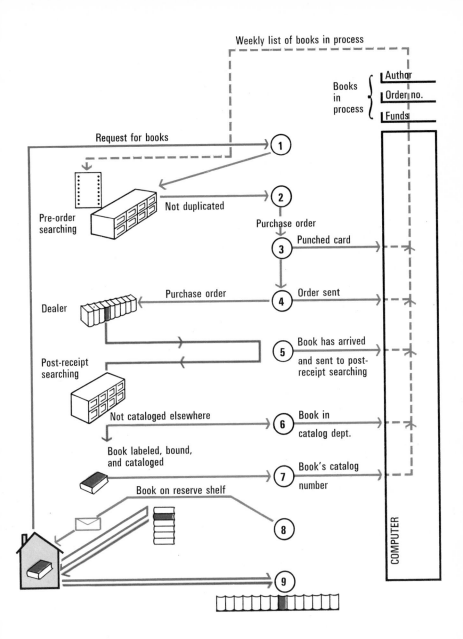

Weekly list of books in process

Books in process { Author, Order no., Funds }

Request for books

1

Pre-order searching

Not duplicated

2

Purchase order

3 Punched card

Dealer

Purchase order

4 Order sent

Post-receipt searching

5 Book has arrived and sent to post-receipt searching

Not cataloged elsewhere

6 Book in catalog dept.

Book labeled, bound, and cataloged

7 Book's catalog number

Book on reserve shelf

8

9

COMPUTER

The Machine Aided Technical Processing System (MATPS) in use at Yale University Library is diagramed above. Basically it makes use of the computer's ability to store, process, and reproduce all the paperwork details associated with ordering books that are not already in stock. As well as speeding up final delivery of books to the library, the system also allows more efficient communication with requesters, greater control over the whole process, and the production of accurate, up-to-date statistics. The movement of the requester is shown in blue, the book in red, and all system communications in green.

library service could not possibly satisfy the information needs of the scientific world—not without outside help. This was realized some time ago in the United States and committees were set up to investigate the growing crisis in scientific and technical information. "Science, Government, and Information" is a report of the President's Science Advisory Committee, whose chairman was Alvin M. Weinberg, the Director of Oak Ridge National Laboratory. It was endorsed by John F. Kennedy in 1963. The difficulty was, and still is, that for science and technology to progress adequately, each scientist must be in touch with his colleagues and the work of his predecessors, and every branch of science must interact with other branches of science. However, as scientific activity grows and diversifies it becomes harder for the literature to remain a unity—that is, to be accessible and comprehensible to all who need it. The danger is that science will fragment into a "mass of repetitious findings, or worse, into conflicting specialties that are not recognized as being mutually inconsistent."

Having made this statement, the report considers how people can decide how far to go in spending time and money on technological communication. How does the head of a Federal Agency (like Alvin Weinberg) decide the appropriate size of his information service? How does a professional society through its publication committee decide whether to embark on a new journal? How does a working scientist decide whether to spend more time in the library? Alas, the most common reaction is to make a weak decision, or none at all, because the whole problem is so intangible. Many scientists have a guilty conscience about not examining as many journals as they believe they should see. Others seem to have lost their conscience; as the Weinberg report puts it: "The anomalies of our information system have conditioned some scientists to active resistance to being informed." The committee made a number of strong recommendations designed to overcome this. They even made the suggestion that each research scientist would do very well if he spent half his time trying to create new scientific information and the rest of it digesting other work and communicating his own.

One valuable simplification weaves its way through the report. There are three sorts of people who need to read scientific information—the basic scientist, the technologist, and the technical administrator. The basic scientist, to whom the information dilemma appears fairly remote, confines his interests to a few narrow specialties and "if communication with a neighboring field becomes too difficult, he imperceptibly narrows his interest to those matters on which he believes he can keep himself informed." At the other extreme, is the technologist. "He cannot afford the luxury of accommodating the size of his field of interest to what his information system can handle. His job is to design a rocket, or a communication system, or a reactor, and his customer will not be satisfied with inadequate design because some knowledge was out of his field." Thirdly, the technical administrator requires something different again called "scientific intelligence," including what is being done by whom, and who is available for doing what. At every level of management, scientific intelligence is used by the administrator when he draws up a research program, proposes a new project, or decides to cut back on an old one.

A very apposite suggestion in the report is the idea of a switching system. This might be analogous to a telephone network with its "forward switching" technique, but it may achieve reality in association with some future "store and forward" data communication network, as we shall find in Chapter 6. The report points out that the information process comprises separate steps: generation, recording and exposition, cataloging, storage and dissemination, study and exploitation by the user. The first two steps and the last two— generation and recording and exposition, as well as study and exploitation—are performed by scientists and technologists. The intermediate steps are performed by professional documentalists, and organizations that handle information. This information chain operates like a switching system. The ultimate aim is to connect the user, quickly and efficiently, to the proper information so far as it is possible to define in advance the proper information.

With this analogy it is easy to see that what limits the information flow is the capacity of the user to absorb information. "Evidence is accumulating that the amount of scientific literature the user will pay attention to is limited; one survey conducted by Biological Abstracts suggests that on the average a biologist can scan journals or titles or abstracts involving 5000 papers per year. Thus the information switching system, to be effective, must be more than a passive switch: it must select, compact, and review material for the individual user so that he *actually assimilates* what he is exposed to, and he is not exposed to too much that is unimportant or irrelevant. Its fundamental task is switching of *information*, not documents."

Future Library Services

The Weinberg report was the signal for a great spurt in American scientific documentation. Its "Recommendations to Government Agencies" are being carried out: there are already a number of specialist national information centers, as we have seen; there are even more reports by systems analysts, and plans reaching well into the 1970s. Its "Recommendations to the Technical Community" are themselves a vision of the way information services are developing. First of all technical libraries will undergo an improvement in status: "The technical community must recognize that handling of technical information is a worthy and integral part of science," and "Techniques of handling information must be widely taught." Both these recommendations are bearing fruit, for new schools of documentation and librarianship are being founded within the higher education systems of many countries, and existing schools are expanding; and the technical community is employing their ex-students directly or indirectly.

Technology is devising improvements within the traditional framework of library usage. Take, for example, the time needed by a user to find a document, once he has retrieved a card with its bibliographic description. This time-delay can be drastically reduced if the card also contains the document—

in microfilm form. The necessary camera and viewer must be engineered with high precision, but ideally the user can in a few seconds project an image of his document on to a viewing screen and proceed to read it page by page, turning a knob for each page change.

Traditional library services are not enough, for "the technical community must explore and exploit new switching methods." The kinds of methods put forward for linking up the library user with the right documents are:

(a) *Specialized information centers:* There should be more of these, and they should be in the charge of professional working scientists and engineers because of their ability to maintain the closest contact with the technical professions.

(b) *Central depositories:* Authors submit their manuscripts to a depository, which announces them and distributes them to all who ask for them. This system overcomes much of the delay in publication by traditional methods, which without priority treatment will usually be more than a year.

(c) *Mechanized information processing:* This includes the use of computers, and "graphical" devices that display documents for human reading. It is too big a question for a small report, but one peep into the future has set the publishing world astir. "The invention of the new retrieval methods is beginning to affect our traditional modes of communication. The traditional forms of book, journal, and reprint may eventually give way to the machine storage of graphical and digital information and machine-generated copy. The technical publishing business may gradually be transformed into the *information handling* business in which the printing press as a means of mass production of identical documents no longer plays a dominant role." In Chapter 6 we shall see how it is even now feasible that a scientist could walk into a library and read an article which exists, not in that library nor in any other, but as a single unique copy in digital form, accessible through a central computer many miles away.

(d) *Development of software:* Much expert thought and effort is needed to make the best use of computers for analyzing and indexing documents, and controlling large stores of library information. Since labor of this sort bears fruit in the form of computer programs, it is said to be concerned with "software," as opposed to hardware that is the computer itself and its peripheral equipment.

The report looks on the American scientific information system as a network of separate subsystems, and asks for uniformity and compatibility in them, because rapid and efficient switching between the different elements is essential. This is obviously true for every developing and every established industrial country, and indeed for the world as a whole.

A look into the future thus seems to offer much reassurance to our hard pressed technical libraries. At present they are struggling to improve their services and to persuade their customers that they should take more advantage of them. They have the Gilbertian task of convincing scientists that they are ill-informed, while begging them to say what information they need. The future will bring a much better appreciation by scientists generally of what libraries can do, and a sharing by them of the burden. Technology will be brought in to assist libraries and add to their usefulness. Special libraries and information centers will be more accessible. Funds will be provided for communication equipment and the traditional custodianship of books and their addresses will be only one of a widening set of responsibilities.

The Market Place

When books were rare, and writing was even slower than publishing is today, men exchanged opinions and ideas in the market place, and probably this means of communication was as effective in the circumstances as our much more versatile methods are in the complex conditions of modern life. If this chapter has given the impression that the only means of scientific communication is through the printed word and the library, and we are in danger of suffocation under a confusing jumble of documents, it is time to let in some fresh air.

The modern basic scientist has an excellent means of talking to his fellow experts from all over the world, now that travel is so cheap and easy, at the conference or symposium. In many subjects this is an annual event, attended each time by different representatives from a high proportion of the interested laboratories. Papers are prepared by those who have something new to say, and they may well be incomplete since they may have to be written six months before the meeting. They will at least contain an account of the aims and the method, and some preliminary results. They will be duplicated and sent to all participants, who will be able to give reasoned comments at the time of the symposium, when the author of a paper may also be able to add details of results. In this way the time lag between any important development and its being known and understood in many other laboratories is often very short indeed; but this system only works well for new and rather grandiose information. Of course communication continues afterwards by correspondence and visits.

The technologist benefits, too, from these international gatherings, either by attending himself or through the scientists who advise him. Similarly the administrator learns "what is being done by whom," but it must be admitted that in the regions of development remote from that of pure science there are still many examples of two groups of people working on similar projects in complete ignorance of each other. Unfortunately for every known example of this magnitude, there must be thousands of smaller or more detailed ideas that are never properly passed around through difficulties of verbal communication. Patents, of which there are over 200,000 per year, are one example where the printed word it vital; but now we are back in the central problem of library information retrieval, which will be further discussed in Chapter 4. The art of current awareness, our nearest documentalistic substitute for the classical market place, will be considered in Chapter 5.

4   Classification and Description

What is information retrieval, and in particular what is library information? In the last resort, it is something very personal, very subjective, as the following example will show.

A certain British projecting device, called a *Belshazzar*, is used in teaching and lecturing to cast on a screen or wall whatever is depicted on its transparent table. As the lecturer writes on the transparency, an enlarged shadow of his hand and its writing appears on the wall behind him. Someone might be struck by the curious name of this projector, and go to a library to find whether there could be a reason for it. Here, very likely, a librarian might be able to tell him the answer at once. Alternatively he could look up the word *Belshazzar* in a large dictionary or an encyclopedia, and find it to be the biblical version of the name of a Babylonian king. Hot on the scent, he would now find a Bible and learn from its concordance that Belshazzar is mentioned in the Book of Daniel. Finally, in Chapter 5 of the Book of Daniel, he finds the story of Belshazzar's feast with the ominous writing on the wall.

This is a view inside a U.S. Patents Office. When a new patent is submitted, the records must be searched to avoid duplication of ideas. This is a very thorough search of a well-organized collection of careful descriptions of previous patents. This chapter considers the difficulty of describing the contents of documents and of classifying them in this and other types of collections.

He is now satisfied that he has the information he wants, because almost certainly the manufacturer had this story in mind when he gave the appliance its name. However, he has found out plenty of additional information, over and above what he really wanted, thus:

(1) the shelf address of the dictionary or encyclopedia with a reference to Belshazzar;

(2) all that he read about other matters before finding the reference to Belshazzar;

(3) the address of a Bible with a concordance;

(4) the address of Daniel Chapter 5 within the Bible;

(5) all that he read about Belshazzar before he came to the verses about the writing on the wall (and probably a whole lot more, including Daniel haranguing the king and finally reading and interpreting the writing to him).

How much of this information was necessary, and how much was worthwhile? Obviously it is hard to pin it down, and yet the enquirer is assuredly satisfied with the information he has found. Some of the information (like the position of the book on the shelf) was perhaps not worth remembering, and some was of continuing value, but where one sort ends and the other begins is hard to decide. Equally hard is the task of devising any kind of measurement to use as a guide in choosing the best method of retrieval.

In choices like these, human judgment usually takes over from scientific measurement; and one of the factors in human judgment is the behavior of other people. Conscientious librarians continually worry about how well their library is doing its job, and they have to base their opinion on such indicators as customer satisfaction, number of subscribers, and comparison with other libraries. These are perfectly reasonable criteria—most reviews of quality are made on this basis, from hairdressing to typewriter manufacture, from automobiles to banking services; but in the case of libraries there are several drawbacks. The quality of one library cannot be compared with another as easily as one might compare one swimsuit, or even one travel agency, with another. Moreover, suppose someone has invented a machine that will print extracts from books in answer to enquiries put into it but that costs a million dollars to buy and another large sum to maintain and operate. How is any library to decide whether or not to invest its money in such a machine? Decide they must, but no reference to their customer records will help them.

Reverting to Belshazzar, we might ask whether this is a typical example of information retrieval. In a way it is, though a rather easy one. It is a great help to have for the main clue a proper name, and an unusual one at that. When the only clues are as general as "wall," "moving finger," "shadow," and "writing" it is very much harder to begin the search and, in the event of failure, to know when it is finished. One extremely common form of search that is similar to our example, but in which the searcher hopes to fail rather than to succeed, is the patent search. When an inventor wants to take out a patent, he has to claim that his idea is novel and to state where the novelty lies. He pays a fee toward the cost of searching the records of all previous patents, and if this search fails to reveal that the novelty has already been claimed by someone else, the inventor is a happy man. Needless to say, this must be an exceptionally thorough search, to prevent any trouble and expense that might arise if, later on, another inventor claims that his patent has been infringed. Nevertheless, the patent search is in principle the same as the lighthearted hunt for Belshazzar except that, instead of depending on two familiar books, the searcher checks a well-organized set of extremely careful descriptions of all previous patents. Here, in contrast to the library search, the distinction between relevant and irrelevant information is clear-cut. A patent description is relevant if it contradicts a claim of novelty; if not, it is irrelevant.

The Belshazzar search is also reasonably typical of many searches that are made in general and scientific literature. The inquirer already knows something, and wants to read books or other documents that will tell him more. He therefore describes to himself or to a librarian the appropriate part of what he knows. What he wants to know is an extension of this description. He then examines documents, or titles or other descriptions of them, and decides whether they are likely to help him.

In general, they are most likely to help if they have a lot in common with the description of what he wants to know. In our simple example, all they need to have in common is the one word, *Belshazzar*.

Library Classification

In the last chapter we saw that the classification system is a key part of the main library system. Here it will be considered as something desirable in itself, because it increases understanding in an extremely powerful manner. By insisting on associations within classes of items it leads us, as it were, along paths in the undergrowth of knowledge; but, because it is easier to follow old paths than to make new ones, it sometimes misleads us and we fail to see new associations that would help us on our way. There are many possible library classifications. How does any one of them come about?

Consider the following problem. A librarian is presented with a mile of books, all new, and a mile of shelves. Without marking them in any way, but with the help of any system or rules that he cares to choose, he arranges the books according to subject along the shelves. He then removes one book from the shelves, and closes the gap. He takes the book and a copy of his system to a colleague, and asks him to put it back on the shelves. What are the chances that the colleague will put the book back in the place that it came from? Not very rosy, on the whole. Sometimes he will be exactly right, and sometimes within a foot or two of the right place; but all too often he will be hundreds of yards away. As a result, anyone wanting that particular book who interpreted the rules in the same way as the original librarian would not find it. Luckily this situation does not arise in practice because libraries do put shelf addresses on books, and they arrange matters so that if the author's name is known there is no difficulty in finding a book.

Unfortunately something rather similar to the above situation arises quite frequently, and it is extremely difficult to prevent. Consider a man with an inquiry. He borrows a copy of the system and arranges his inquiry according to subject just as if it were another book. He then walks to the appropriate part of the shelves and hopes to find there the books answering his inquiry. He will probably find some of the relevant books, but others will be scattered to the far ends of the shelves and he will never find them. It may be argued that the books in answer to an inquiry may be found in other ways besides walking along the shelves. Traditionally, their titles, authors' names, and often some idea of their contents may be found in classified indexes or in bibliographies—either those prepared by specialist librarians or those occurring at the ends of chapters in ordinary books. However, these alternatives are not fundamentally different from the mile of books. Whatever form a classified index takes, it is equivalent to many drawers full of cards, each card describing one book and containing its shelf address; the cards are arranged in the drawers in an order according to a classification of their own (this is most often the same as the shelf classification of the books). Similarly, in professional bibliographies the book titles are arranged in a carefully chosen order, use being made of a classification system. We shall call these *linear* classifications because of their analogy with the linear arrangement of books along shelves. The point to be understood here is that every linear classification presents the books or their titles to an inquirer one at a time in a definite linear sequence, and hence no linear classification is likely to provide in a single subsection the complete set of books answering an inquiry.

Nevertheless, conventional libraries must arrange their books, actually or by proxy, in a definite order and the various systems and rules they use for classifying books are well worth studying. Any practical system has many virtues. It provides for tidiness, reducing the danger of a book being lost on the shelves. The classification order turns up again and again: on the shelves, in the card index, in the collection of dockets representing books that are out on loan. As we have just seen, it makes a useful device by which the inquirer can frame his inquiry, by virtue of the notion that an inquiry is the same sort of thing as a book and can be classified in the same way. And although the system will not give perfect retrieval, it goes some way toward it—far enough for many ordinary purposes.

As we saw in Chapter 3, classification is simply the description in a special language of a book or document and of the set of classes to which it can be assigned. "Classify and describe" is only a variation on Julius Caesar's "Divide and rule." A classification system provides an order in which books and index cards can be stored. Because men have written down almost all they know, a good classification must have a slot for the name or description of every object and idea in the universe, including those yet to be discovered. This makes classifying sound heroic, but it can be very humdrum and at times utterly exasperating. Classification is the basis of librarianship—as well as of botany, archaeology, and many other sciences—and although much has been said, written, and done in its name it still suffers from having no truly acceptable and authoritative account. The Hercules who will clean out these particular stables has not yet emerged.

There are scores of conventional classification systems in use in libraries today. These range from the intricate Universal Decimal Classification (UDC)—revised by the British Standards Institution in 1948 and widely used in both general and scientific libraries—to the Library of Congress Classification devised at the turn of the century, and the multiple classifications of hierarchical, faceted, and coordinate systems. The important questions from our point of view are: how well do they work in practice, what are their special merits, and are they capable of being mechanized? Let us look at four typical ones and then consider how computers and other mechanical aids can be used in conjunction with these and other simpler classification systems to speed up the whole business of library information retrieval.

Linear Classification

Linear, as opposed to multiple, classifications are used to arrange books in relation to their primary interest. In the Universal Decimal Classification every book has on its spine a number, carefully worked out and put there by a librarian. For example, a book whose title is *Telecommunication* and another book called *Messages Across the World*, if we assume

| 621.36 | 621.38 | 621.39 | 621.41 | 621.43 | 621.44 |

Thermoelectricity / Various scientific apparatus, discharge tubes / Telecommunications / Hot-air engines / Internal combustion engines / Engines using vapor mixtures

The above diagram shows how books may be grouped according to the Universal Decimal Classification (UDC), which is used in many libraries and is fully described in the text. As can be seen, some of these categories are related to neighboring ones (so forming a browsing area), but others are quite distinct.

that their titles faithfully describe their contents, will both be numbered 621.39 and will stand side by side on the shelf. Each digit of this number has an interpretation as follows:

6 in the first place: Applied sciences
2 in the second place: Engineering sciences
1 before the point: Mechanical and Electrical engineering
3 after the point: Electrical engineering
9 second after the point: Telecommunication

The numbers to the left have a higher status than those to the right. All the books on telecommunication are meant to be included among the books on electrical engineering; applied sciences include engineering sciences; and so on. But the numbering of equals is arbitrary: there is no particular reason why 621 Mechanical and Electrical engineering should come before 622 Mining, for instance.

For each of the numbers in the classification system for which he has books, the librarian leaves a space on the shelves, and when the books are in place the numbers on their spines are in numerical order. To accommodate the books, as yet unknown, that will be acquired in the future, the librarian leaves plenty of gaps at random.

If he stocks a lot of books on telecommunication, his clients will be confused by finding they all have the same number. The UDC takes care of this contingency by the addition of further numbers, for example:

6 before the second point:	Radiocommunication
6 after the second point:	Apparatus and Circuits
1 second after the second point	Transmitters, Oscillators, Resonators, Oscillatory circuits
1 before the third point:	Oscillatory circuit characteristics
3 after the third point:	Coupled circuits

Thus, a book called *Circuit Techniques for Coupling and Mixing TV Signals* would be numbered 621.396.611.3, if the classifier thought that its main interest was coupled circuits.

When Melvil Dewey, in 1875, wrote an account of the classification system he had invented for the Amherst College Library, Massachusetts, and submitted it as the thesis for his Master's degree, it ran to only 24 pages of printed material. The UDC system was founded on it, and the 1942 edition contained 1929 pages.

It will be obvious that many man-years of reading, sifting, thinking, and testing must have gone into the design of the UDC and of any comparable system. After all, 621.396.611.3 is a ten-digit number, which suggests that there are up to 10^{10} or 10,000,000,000 different classes. These cannot possibly have been individually thought about, for a man thinking of a class every second would have to think for 100,000 days, or about 300 years, to produce so many; and, besides, we should need at least 100 times as many books as we have now, to put one in every class. Nevertheless, we can begin to visualize how a man-made classification system can grow into being, particularly when it is directed by a man as capable as Dr. Herbert Putnam, who organized the Library of Congress Classification from about 1899 onward. (Before this time it was very rudimentary indeed.) Dr. Putnam is credited in Berwick Sayers' book *An Introduction to Library Classification* with the best definition of the work of the professional classifier, namely:

"The books are roughly divided by main classes, as History, Economics, Art, Music, Mathematics, Physics, Chemistry, etc., and distributed to the classifiers for assigning to the special subjects. The classifier ascertains for each book:

(a) The main subject from the author's point of view and from the nature of the contents—sometimes at variance with the language of the title-page.

(b) The main subject from the standpoint of the library (e.g. in a theological library the history of a parish will be classified with church history; in a general library it may be of more value with other histories of the place).

(c) The place of that subject in the scheme of classification in use. This an expert classifier usually knows without recourse to the alphabetical index of subjects, but in many cases a glance at a shelf-list or at the books themselves on the shelves is necessary to make sure that the book in hand agrees with the evident character of the other books classified there."

The general opinion is that Putnam's methods have led to a classification of the highest integrity, well suited to the purposes of congressmen and of American administrators, and fairly suitable for the general public who also use the Library of Congress. Its weakness—the chronic weakness of all linear classifications—is the inadequacy of step (b). Instead of the standpoint of the library (whatever that means), the classifier should be thinking of the standpoints of all the individuals who are likely to use the library and to need the book he has in his hand. This he cannot do, and those customers whose standpoints do not conform must suffer accordingly.

The classifier who uses a linear system may notice that some books have a secondary interest—for example, a book about colour may be primarily chemistry but secondarily history of art. He can then reclassify it from the second point of view. The usual practice, if he does so, is not to buy a second copy of the book and place it at a different shelf address, but to make out a second index card showing the new classification number and the original shelf address. Finding secondary classifications is of course time-consuming, and still falls far short of representing the standpoint of all conceivable users.

Multiple Classifications

The librarians of the past had ideas other than the linear

systems into which they were naturally forced by their book-shelves and their lists. For example, they used hierarchical systems, to which we shall come shortly. They no doubt looked at the way other scholars were classifying un-booklike objects such as stars, plants, animals, fossils, and rocks. If they had foreseen the properties of electronic computers, they would have looked still harder. There is nothing linear or shelf-like about a core store: for example, by its wiring any particular core is found by three numbers, two defining the row and column of the core in its matrix plane, and the third defining which matrix plane it is in. Thus, as we have seen in Chapter 2, core stores and magnetic disks and drums have the facility known as *random access*. Any piece of information stored in binary form in such a store—for example, the shelf address of a book—can be located and read out very quickly indeed. This means that although librarians have to store their books linearly, they can store their shelf addresses and other particulars in any way they like, provided a computer is available.

What ways are there of arranging a store of index information? This question applies not only to libraries but to any sort of index and to any problem of classification, so some of the examples in the next section will be drawn from other activities besides librarianship. A convenient way of illustrat-

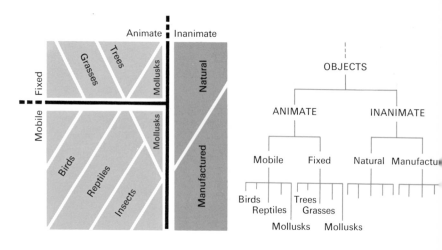

ing the more elaborate ways of classification is to represent classes by areas. Such illustrations are called *Venn diagrams* and are used in set theory and Boolean algebra. The diagram opposite shows a classification of objects that have a special property. (All possible kinds of objects are supposed to be represented within the square.) The vertical black line that divides the whole area in two is well-defined—it divides inanimate from animate objects. So, too, are other lines, but not all of them. By paying attention to all the well-defined lines, the family tree shown next to it can be drawn. It is called a *hierarchical classification,* and most libraries use a system that is at least partly hierarchical. The example on page 87 shows that the UDC classification is hierarchical: having decided that the book in question was in the realm of applied sciences, the next step down the hierarchy was what section of applied sciences (engineering sciences); and the step after that was what aspect of engineering sciences; and so on. Notice, however, that in the present example "mollusks" are divided willy-nilly into "mobile" and "fixed." If this classification were used for the shelf order of books, the order would go (leaving out the higher levels): birds, reptiles, insects, mollusks, grasses, trees, mollusks. Clearly there are traps and absurdities to be wary about.

The diagram at far left shows how classes may be represented with areas to form a hierarchical classification. The family tree, drawn by observing all well-defined lines, emphasizes its hierarchical nature. At right an area is divided to form a faceted classification. Here, in contrast to the diagram at far left, each dividing line cuts through all the areas formed by the other dividing lines.

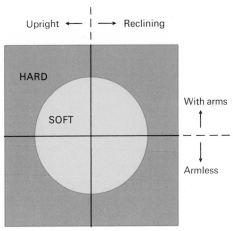

The diagram on page 91 is an introduction to another special way of dividing up an area that is receiving a great deal of attention from librarians. It is a very simple, and therefore untypical, example of *faceted classification*. Not only is each dividing line well defined, but it also cuts through all the areas formed by the other dividing lines. In the figure, the whole field represents all kinds of chairs, and the assumption is made that any chair must be upright or reclining, with arms or armless, and hard or soft. This system immediately produces eight classes of chairs. Further classes can be made by subdividing any of the eight areas, and if the same criteria are applied to all (e.g. made in Europe, America, Asia, etc.) the faceting evidently goes a stage further. Each type of division (such as "hard or soft") is called by librarians a *facet*, and there can be more than two alternatives in a facet. Thus a division might be used with the choices "hard," "soft with springs," and "soft without springs," and it could be represented in the figure with the help of an extra concentric circle. We shall call each choice in a classification a *descriptor*, and shall next demonstrate the remarkable economy in descriptors of a faceted classification.

The diagram opposite is of a faceted classification with more than two descriptors in most of the facets. It was actually used by an opinion poll, in which the subject classified was the population of the United Kingdom—and the pollsters may be surprised to see their method described in terms of descriptors and facets. Recently the *Observer*, a London Sunday paper, published the result of an opinion poll on the hypothetical question "Who would you choose to be President of Great Britain?" The overall results gave first place to the queen's husband, the Duke of Edinburgh, but our present interest is the way chosen to break down the voting population. The breakdown produced no less than 240 classes of voter, and it was achieved with only 4 facets, having 4, 5, 6, and 2 descriptors respectively, namely a total of 17 descriptors. Even this is not the most economical way to use facets and descriptors. Maximum effectiveness is obtained by having exactly 3 descriptors for each facet. Thus, taking a simple

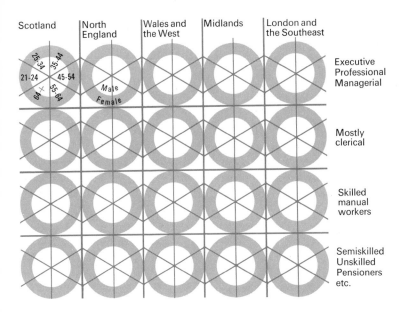

The above diagram shows how the population of the United Kingdom was divided up for the interpretation of results from an opinion poll (see text). The faceted classification used contained 4 facets, having 4, 5, 6, and 2 descriptors respectively, to produce 240 classes.

problem of using 12 descriptors to make as many classes as possible, we find

      6 facets of 2 descriptors each make 2^6 or 64 classes

      4 facets of 3 descriptors each make 3^4 or 81 classes

      3 facets of 4 descriptors each make 4^3 or 64 classes

      2 facets of 6 descriptors each make 6^2 or 36 classes

It would be false to suppose that hierarchical classification tells you more about a book than faceting, simply because the total number of descriptors is larger. The diagram on page 94 shows a very simple case of each, in which the answer to any question must be either Yes or No, with equal probability. Consider an object classified as a ★ by the hierarchy on the left. The four relevant questions were 1, 2, 4, and 8, and their answers were Yes, Yes, Yes, No. The remaining questions— 3, 5, 6, 7, 9, 10, 11, 12, 13, 14, and 15—were not asked, because

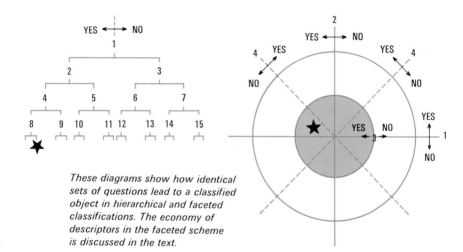

These diagrams show how identical sets of questions lead to a classified object in hierarchical and faceted classifications. The economy of descriptors in the faceted scheme is discussed in the text.

they were not relevant. There was 1 chance in 16 of getting that particular set of 4 answers, and the information, using the formula from Chapter 1, was $-\log_2(1/16)$, namely 4 bits. In the faceted scheme on the right, an object would be put in the class marked ★ if the answers to questions 1, 2, 3, and 4 were again Yes, Yes, Yes, No. Obviously the amount of information is again 4 bits. On counting the descriptors, and remembering that each Yes and each No corresponds to a descriptor, we find that the faceted classification used 8 descriptors against 30 by the hierarchical system, and yet they both yielded the same amount of information.

Facets were discussed in great detail by a gathering of experts in 1957 at a study conference of the Fédération Internationale de Documentation, and among their conclusions were:

"(1) The scope of classification. Traditional classification has been concerned with the construction of hierarchies — chains of classes and coordinated arrays. Modern information retrieval techniques also necessitate the combination of terms to express complex subjects. . . .

(2) Schemes of classification. There is general agreement that the most helpful form of classification scheme for in-

formation retrieval is one which groups terms into well-defined categories, which can be used independently to form compounds, and within which the terms can be arranged in hierarchies. . . ." (An example of terms used independently to form compounds might be "Scottish, male, aged 21–4.")

The British Classification Research Group has been very active both before and since that meeting, and it was already working out how to prepare a new, general, encyclopedic scheme of classification incorporating facets. But reaching decisions about facets is an exceptionally difficult task, far harder than deciding on categories in a hierarchy. The meeting's chairman, M. Eric de Grolier, advised them to "wait one or two (we hope it will not be ten) years before we are able to determine exactly on what basis such a scheme must be constructed." By now nearly 12 years have elapsed and the indications are that the warning was more than justified. Limited systems are much easier to devise than a big general scheme, and special libraries such as that of the Metal Box Company have been using faceted systems for up to 10 years. Unfortunately these limited systems cannot be built into a satisfactory general scheme; for this, a separate new start must be made.

The coordinate classification shown below is similar to a faceted system except that modifications can be made in any part without damaging other parts. Areas A, B, and C and the difficulties of using a coordinate classification are described in the text.

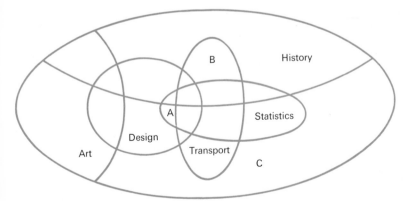

Only one more method of classification will be illustrated. In the diagram on page 95, books are supposed to be classified by asking the five questions "Is it about art/design/transport/ statistics/history?" A book in the area marked A would be about design and statistics, but not art, transport, or history. In area B it would be about history and transport, but none of the others. In area C it would be about a subject not covered by any of the five questions.

Every one of the 20 areas in the figure is appropriate for a different class of book; and we may suppose for the sake of the example that the unrepresented combinations, 12 in all, such as art and statistics, do not occur. This is called a coordinate classification. As in a faceted classification, every item used in it has the same level of importance; but, unlike a faceted classification, additions or modifications can be made in any part of it without damaging other parts. Little skill is needed in devising quite elaborate coordinate systems—in fact, a computer can do it, and an example will be given at the end of the chapter. No doubt there are many private libraries whose shelf arrangement conforms more or less to a coordinate classification; retrieval from them depends mainly on the memory of the owner.

Attitudes to Classification

In these few simple examples it should be evident that devising a classification is not, like building a house, a problem that can be solved by a well-tried method. There are many directions of approach, each of which leaves something to be desired, and none of which can hope to produce a classification that works well on all occasions. The hierarchical method is a painstaking division of the field into smaller and smaller pieces, each of which has to be considered separately—really quite a welcome restriction—but a typical book or document fits not *one* small piece of the field, but many. Faceted systems are fiendishly difficult to design but economical in the number of key questions to be answered by the indexer, with the hope that there will be reasonable agreement between different indexers. Coordinate systems are so formless that it is difficult to lay down rules for designing them. If they were memorizable, the human brain would form associations of ideas that would turn a mechanical task into an intellectual one. However, they cannot be memorized and are best handled by computers. Provided that a different number is assigned to each half of each facet, faceted systems (and coordinate systems similarly) will determine a shelf order for a collection of books, but it will not be a very good order for browsing.

R. A. Fairthorne, in 1953, wrote some scathing criticisms of the attitudes of librarians who should know better, and they deserve the attention of all who are trying to understand classification. They are incorporated in his book *Towards Information Retrieval* (1961) in the chapter on "Delegation of Classification". His first two paragraphs set the tone:

"Library classifications display lists of labels for texts, but rarely tell how to bestow the right label on the right text. Library classification theory, which aims at telling how to work such labels, is even more coy. Classifying is an act too shameful for mention, and the texts themselves are no better than they ought to be. Conversation is kept clean by talking of, for instance, 'the field of knowledge' when what is meant is at most 'the field of language' and, often, only 'the verbal content of published texts'; by talking of 'concepts' when what is meant, at most, is 'what remains unaltered when a classification schedule is translated' and often 'modes of describing textual content'; and so on.

A heavy price is paid for this prudishness: an underlying belief, the more dangerous for being unacknowledged, in an absolute eternal and unchanging field of ideas which is uncovered bit by bit. A special classification is a map of all that has uncovered itself to date. The classifier, inasmuch as he is mentioned at all, is a discoverer, not an inventor. Any acute and right-minded observer, at any place and at any time and whatever his previous reading, will arrive at the same classification of the same 'idea' or statement or document (it is never quite clear what are the entities under observation)."

What we sometimes forget is that we are classifying the signals from our senses every moment of our waking life.

Even in our sleep we hear a noise, classify it as unusual, and wake up to check that it is only harmless-unusual and not dangerous-unusual. We can bear to live only because 99.9 per cent of the events that happen to us have happened in nearly the same way many times before—we have classified most of them before they have finished happening. Is it not strange that after all this experience we cannot classify a book? Yet it is true, and, facing the fact honestly, we should be clamoring for help from the machine system designers.

How Can Computers Help?

Computers can match words. Suppose a computer store contains a list of words—a "vocabulary"—in a binary code. If any word in the list is put into the computer, with a very simple program the computer will find the position in the list of the matching word, i.e. determine its ordinal number. On this simple beginning a great deal can be built, even though negligible use is made of the computer's arithmetic facilities. All it needs to do is to read, write, match, and count.

If expense does not matter, it is quite credible that a computer could serve as a whole library, librarian and all. What would it have to do?

(1) Store the books and other documents word by word in digital form, using the ordinal number in place of each word. It must then be able to send to the printing device signals representing documents or parts of documents whenever they are required. Thus if the first word required has the number 1234, and the 1234th word in the vocabulary is *cabbage*, it must send signals to the printer that cause it to print *cabbage* in full.

(2) Store the title and a brief description of each document (its *abstract*).

(3) Store the classification of each document (in a special language), together with the address of the stored document and the address of the stored abstract. (The classification is also a very brief description of the document, and can be called a *microabstract*.)

(4) Accept any request in ordinary language for information

through a microphone, a display, a punched paper tape, or some other medium.

(5) Convert the request from ordinary language to the special language used in classification. For this purpose a schedule of the classification system must be stored in the computer.

(6) Find the documents whose classification most nearly matches the request classification.

(7) Print out abstracts and other samples for inspection by the inquirer.

(8) Print out any documents or parts of documents chosen by the inquirer.

The above list is far from being an overstatement of what a computer can do. Indeed, later in this chapter and in chapters 6 and 7 we shall see that it is in many ways an understatement. The reasons why there is no such fully automated library in the world at present are connected with the very high cost and the time needed to get it into operation; but these alone would not have deterred the wealthier countries from taking action. What is really holding them back is the high probability that, before such a library could be finished, technological advances would have made it advisable to scrap the whole project and start again on a much cheaper and better automated system.

In the book *Libraries of the Future*, describing his research project of the early 1960s, J. C. R. Licklider estimates that the world's stock of different books in 1970, if put into a computer store, would need 10^{15} bits of storage space. At 1 dollar per 10,000 bits the store alone would cost $100 million. Another way of expressing the size of the body of knowledge is to imagine it typed in a single line of typing—100,000,000 miles long. The only practical way at present of getting the world's books into a computer store is by keypunching, i.e. using typewriters with a paper tape output. To type that length of message would cost a mere billion dollars.

It is well known that the corpus of printed knowledge is growing exponentially, and its growth factor can be expressed by saying that the corpus doubles itself every 15 to 20 years. But, as Licklider points out, the technology too is growing exponentially and its growth factor is perhaps 10 times as great (i.e. doubling itself about every 2 years). "Moreover, the technology is not yet near any fundamental physical limits to development. Thus in the present century, we may be technically capable of processing the entire body of knowledge in almost any way we can describe. . . ."

We had to take this interim look at automated libraries in order to see classification from a fresh point of view. When a computer can be made to print out abstracts and other samples of documents for inspection by the inquirer, he can find out all he needs to know before deciding which to read. He can be expected to decide well enough without approaching the book-shelves, and therefore the shelf addresses of books need not be assigned with any of the care given in traditional libraries. They must have precise addresses so that they can be found, but they can be next to quite unrelated books; shelf

Information-processing equipment in use at the Chemical Abstracts Service in Columbus, Ohio. Information is typed directly into data-recording devices (seen behind the typewriters) and transmitted as electronic signals into computers. These reorganize the material for computer-directed typesetting for books or journals, and make possible almost instantaneous retrieval of any part of the original information.

positions need carry no semantic information.

In particular, when a computer handles the classified index, shelf position need not be determined by a classification system, and the classification need not be designed to provide simple rules about shelf position. This greater freedom is a particularly valuable relief to scientific and technical people, because their most important literature is in the form not of books, but of periodicals. These—the publications of learned societies, reviews, abstract journals, international specialist journals, and trade journals—cannot be classified in detail because each number contains an assortment of articles differing in subject matter and often in degree of originality and type of interest. Each separate article can be accurately classified but cannot as a rule be torn from the magazine and placed with related articles from other journals. In practice, successive numbers of each periodical are stored together, and most of the importance of their shelf position, from the semantic point of view, is lost anyway.

With computers to help us, then, what new systems of classification are open to consideration? One—which was quite startling to scientists when it was introduced in 1961, though it had been used by lawyers since 1873—is *citation indexing*. Of the articles in scientific and technical journals (those which are intended to have a lasting value), over 80 per cent refer to the published work of other authors. Some of these citations may be because of their general interest, but many are given in explanation and acknowledgment of the sources that inspired the article, and thus accurately describe its contents. Any two articles whose citations are similar will have much subject matter in common. Authors of contemporary articles will almost certainly be interested to read about each other's work and perhaps become acquainted and discuss their work on a personal basis. Citation indexing is relatively cheap and easy, using computers and modern methods of storage, and it has been operated commercially for a number of years. Strictly speaking, it is not a system of classification, because it does not put articles into definite classes. It is more accurately described as a system for detecting associations between articles, with a view to retrieval. It operates without any help from expert classifiers.

To see how a citation index works in practice, suppose we require to know what publications in 1967 referred to faceted classification. We begin by thinking of an author of an earlier article that is likely to be cited by anyone who wrote in 1967 about faceting. B. C. Vickery is such an author, particularly in his books *Classification and Indexing in Science* and *On Retrieval System Theory*. His books are on record in the four volumes of the *Citation Index* for 1967 as having been cited by nine authors of papers published in journals—one British, one Russian, and five American journals. Which of these papers discuss faceting? The next step is to retrieve the titles of the nine papers, which for technical reasons are recorded in another set of four volumes. As it happens, none of the titles includes the word *facet*, but two look very promising—the Russian one by Kushul, A. Y., on "The Classification Research Group of England in dealing with some universal classification problems," and an American one by Elias, A. W., on "Indexing in and for technical information centers." All nine documents would now be sent for, but these two would be examined first and most eagerly.

A rather more obvious clue on the subject matter of a document is its title, and in particular the keywords in its title. Keywords can be used as a simple and useful guide for selecting articles on particular subjects; and the computer, with its ability to rearrange and print out words, plays an important part in such *cyclic title indexing*, often erroneously called permuted title indexing. Its commercial sponsors call it the KWIC index—standing for KeyWord In Context. The titles and references of all articles in a selected set of periodicals (one week's or one month's output) are punched onto paper tape and fed into the computer, which has previously been supplied with a vocabulary of keywords. On demand the computer prints out the titles and references again with the keywords in capitals and in alphabetical order. Copies of the printed list are sent to all subscribers. If a title contains five keywords it is printed out at five different places in the alpha-

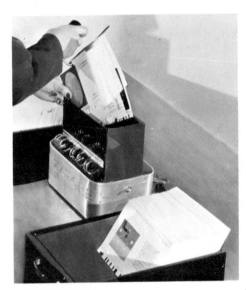

The Calvin Mooers Zatacode system mentioned in the text is shown in use at right. Cards are edge-notched in coded positions according to the information they contain. To search for material on a particular subject (or combination of subjects), rods are inserted into the empty shaker box in appropriate positions and the cards are inserted notches downward. The box is shaken and those cards with notches in at least the positions coded for (and thus satisfying the requirements) fall down about ¾ in. Those sticking up (and thus not suitable) can be lifted away as shown. This system can be very effective for certain collections, and has led to many other ideas on similar lines.

betical list. In the example, only two articles are represented, without their author and journal:

BRIDLE-WAYS   MOTORCYCLE SCRAMBLES on

MAPPING simplified   SURVEYING and

MOTORCYCLE SCRAMBLES on BRIDLE-WAYS

SCRAMBLES on BRIDLE-WAYS   MOTORCYCLE

SURVEYING and MAPPING simplified

The titles are cycled and each keyword in turn is brought to the front. Thus, a person interested in map-making would look out all titles in the list whose first three letters were MAP and among them would find the second entry in the five above, together with a reference to the journal where he could read the complete articles. Cyclic title indexing, like citation indexing, is a guide to retrieval rather than a conventional classification system. It operates without help from professional classifiers, thereby saving time and money.

There are many different ways of giving a reasonable title

to a book or article, even using totally different sets of words. In cyclic title indexes, the inquirer must be alive to this fact and use his own judgment. In libraries using the rather old-fashioned systems of book classification by title, placing the books on the shelves in alphabetical order of title, the professional classifier lends a helping hand. He provides an alphabetical list of possible titles or parts of titles, to each of which is attached a short list of alternative or related titles. As this procedure proves cumbersome, he may make a shorter set of subjects and rename each book with a word from this set. Unfortunately he soon finds himself using two or more such words in the new name; for example, a book about Maxwell's wave equations might have to be renamed *Electromagnetic—waves—propagation—equations*. In consequence he too will have to do something like KWIC indexing, and make entries under Electromagnetic (waves), Waves (electromagnetic), Wave propagation (electromagnetic), and so on. The entries are arranged alphabetically, and the result is often called an *Alphabetical Index*. The set of subjects that he has devised is normally called a *set of descriptors*; each descriptor is not so much a single word as a group of related words all expressing the same idea. Searching an alphabetical index is done by looking for one descriptor at a time, sometimes called *single access*.

Old-fashioned or not, alphabetical indexing is in the direct line of advancement toward mechanical classification of documents as envisaged by present-day research workers, and the first step was to take away the alphabetical arrangement. Calvin Mooers noticed in 1951 that the uniterm or descriptor list of the classifier could be adapted to a simple mechanical way of card sorting, eliminating the need for an alphabetical list altogether. He used knitting needles and edge-notched cards (see the photograph on page 103 of Calvin Mooers Zatocode System). Writing the title and other particulars of a book on a card, he proceeded to put notches in the edge of the card in coded positions, corresponding to the classifier's descriptors for the book. By this means he made a second improvement, obviating the need for single access. The code

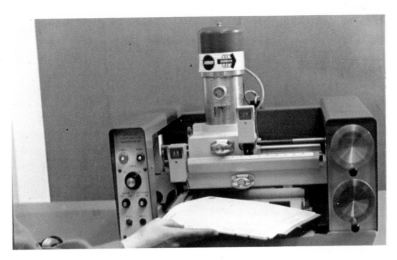

The plastic subject cards used in the optical coincidence equipment shown on this page can be drilled in any of 10,000 separate positions—each representing a reference or book on that subject. The position of each hole is identified by two coordinates seen displayed on the drill above. The reading equipment shown below consists of a light box over which the required subject cards are placed. Holes appearing right through indicate books or documents for which all the chosen categories apply. Their coordinates (and therefore their identity) can be read off using a sliding scale.

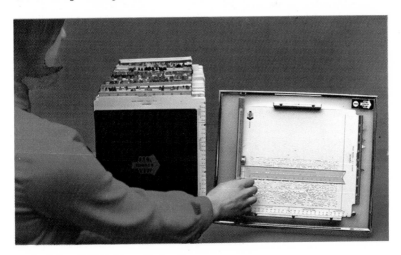

for edge notching was cunningly chosen so that an enormous amount of information can be carried in the edge of an ordinary card without leading to too many "false drops," as he called them. The knitting needles are slightly smaller than the notches and the holes are prepunched near the edge of all cards, waiting to be converted into notches as required. To search for books on a particular subject, simple or compound, all the cards are divided into stacks small enough to go into the box shown in the photograph on page 103. The appropriate hole positions for the required subject are worked out from the code book. Needles are inserted horizontally across the box at just these positions. Each stack of cards is put in, notches downward, and given a good shake; and hey presto!—all the cards with particulars about relevant books drop down $\frac{3}{4}$ in. from the rest of the stack. After use, the cards can be put back in any order without affecting future operations of the system. The system unfortunately failed to attract enough enthusiastic users in the libraries where it was tried, but it demonstrates a welcome escape from the bondage of alphabetical lists and single entries.

Another way of escaping is with an "inverted" file, often implemented as a *peek-a-boo* (or *optical coincidence*) system. A device is made for punching holes precisely in any of, say, 10,000 positions on a large card. Each position is allocated to a book in a library of up to 10,000 books. A separate card is taken for each of the descriptors used by the classifier and, if a particular descriptor is used for one of the books the card has a hole punched in the place appropriate for the book. When all the descriptor cards have been punched for all their relevant books, it is quite simple to search for all books having, for example, the same three descriptors. Let us pick those relating to the ideas "space-time," "invariance," and "velocity of light." The three descriptor cards are taken and stacked together, and held up to the light. Wherever a hole appears right through, its position indicates a book for which those three descriptors are correct (see the photographs on page 105). For the example chosen, the books indicated ought to include books about Einstein's Theory of Relativity.

The peek-a-boo method has proved to be viable, in spite

of its drawback that the number of documents in a searchable group is only equal to the number of distinct positions at which holes can be punched in a card. Using, say, 10 such groups, a library of 100,000 documents can be accommodated; and this number may be increased if cards are replaced by *microfiches*. These are mounted flat films, the size of postcards, that contain microphotographs of pages, and can be assembled in accurately positioned matrices to permit perhaps 100,000 positions on a single sheet. One firm alone claims to have made 1500 installations of optical coincidence equipment in the United Kingdom and America; but any enthusiast with his own small library can make his own set of peek-a-boo cards, the only special equipment required being a positionally accurate punching device.

The inverted file idea can be easily adapted for a computer store, but it leads to a rather rigid system that is difficult to bring up to date as new documents enter the library. The Chemical Abstracts Research Unit at Nottingham University is incorporating inverted files for general logical searches through magnetic tape.

The claim made earlier about the mechanical classification of documents still remains to be substantiated. Can we really dispense with the highly skilled classifiers, quietly working away in the remote recesses of our leading libraries? Can we offer any substitute at all for their judgment, when, for instance, they decide to introduce a new keyword into the system, or when they make tests of user satisfaction? The answer seems likely to be Yes, but strictly speaking, the mechanical task performed will not be classification. It will be a completely brainless identification of keywords and phrases in a keypunched version of the document, combined with a computer scan of a list of keywords in a set of descriptors. As with cyclic title indexing, and indeed with alphabetical indexing, documents are not put strictly into classes. The nearest thing to a class statement takes the form "The document whose title is so-and-so has descriptors 84, 728, and 818." Only in truly alphabetical indexing will there be a meaningful name for descriptor 84 and all the others.

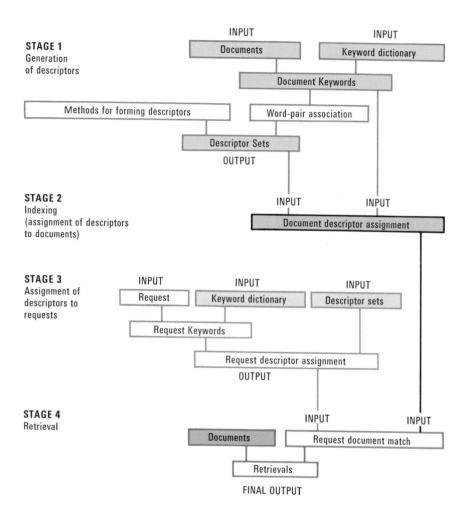

The above diagram shows the essential stages in a mechanical retrieval system devised by Dr. P. K. T. Vaswani of the U.K.'s National Physical Laboratory. The system for retrieving documents from a small library, uses descriptors generated by a computer storing details of over 10,000 documents. These descriptors, mainly of 3 to 10 words, have been very successful in tests under various conditions. Items overlaid by full tone are retained for future use. The set of words shown opposite were selected by a method similar to Vaswani's from a school textbook on elementary geometry.

bisect 1
equidistant

revolve 2
turn

multiply 3
product

great 4
less

face 5
trihedral

diagonal 6
parallelogram

apply 7
coincide
fall
include
position
represent

add 8
sum
contain
rectangle
square

diameter 9
semicircle
right angle
perpendicular
hypotenuse

alternate 10
exterior
interior
opposite
parallel

angle 11
vertical
concyclic
orthocenter
vertex
segment

external 12
internal
figure
ratio
area
part

proportional 13
equiangular
rectilinear
similar
correspond
side
hypothesis

contact 14
circle
inscribe
tangent

touch 15
stand
circumference
divide
radius
center

altitude 16
base
triangle

arc 17
chord

straight line 18
plane
cut
intersect
section
lie

given 19
construct
draw

produce 20
together
adjacent

We have already used the word *descriptor* for a particular choice in a classification, and for an individual keyword. If we now think of a descriptor as consisting of a set of keywords, we must ask what property binds particular keywords in a set. When the alphabetical index classifier was having difficulties a few pages back, he said that a certain book was, among other things, about propagation. He would probably say the same about other books, if they had words like *transmission, delivery, communication*, and even perhaps *gospel* and *message*, in their title. The above words might well be lumped together with others like them to make a descriptor set. A document that used any of the words from the set (or perhaps any two, or any three) could be marked with the name or number of the descriptor. This can obviously be done with a computer, and indeed it has been done already in experimental systems. The only service required from the classifier is at the beginning, when he classifies words by putting them into sets.

The first important classifier of words was P. M. Roget of London, and he called the book containing his list of descriptors *A Thesaurus of English Words and Phrases* (published in 1852). *Thesaurus*, derived from the name of ancient Greek treasure houses such as those at Delphi, has found a new lease of life, and descriptor schedules are often called *thesauri*. People have tried, without much practical success, to use Roget's *Thesaurus* for classifying documents, but the preference now is for sets of descriptors tailor-made for the job. Alas, the professional classifier may after all become redundant, because descriptors can be generated completely mechanically. Dr. P. K. T. Vaswani, at the National Physical Laboratory, England, has programmed a computer to produce sets of descriptors, having first stored a suitable number (over 10,000) of documents. The computer makes a statistical study of the co-occurrence of all possible pairs of words in the same document. Certain pairs, such as "wave-radio," occur together far more often than they would by pure chance, and the computer assembles all such pairs for further treatment. If, for example, "radio-coupling" and "wave coupling" are also strongly associated pairs, the computer may treat the three words as a descriptor set or part of such a set. Operating with machine-generated descriptors mainly of 3 to 10 words, Dr. Vaswani has made a fully mechanical retrieval system for a small library and evaluated its performance under various conditions. (See the flow diagram on page 108.) It copes well with the special problems of searching collections of documents—rather than books, which are more nearly the province of an intelligent librarian in a small library. Its performance with much larger collections will be worth testing.

Shown on page 109 are the descriptors selected by a pilot program fairly similar to Vaswani's, when it was given as data a school textbook on elementary geometry. Clearly the words in each of the 20 descriptor sets have a lot in common, but it would not be easy to give any one of the 20 a name. Here is an obvious difference from descriptors generated by rational thinking, such as those of Roget's *Thesaurus*: the machine-generated descriptors cannot be given a name because they have not originated from a unifying concept. Hence they are difficult for librarians and others to memorize. However this is quite unimportant in practice, when the searching is done by a machine.

If it turns out that descriptors for the contents of a document can be both selected and applied by a computer, we shall have reached an epoch in the development of libraries, comparable with the invention of printing. The nagging worry that haunts some of us—over irretrievably lost information, and duplication of effort—will recede, and we shall no longer fear that ogre, the document explosion.

LE
JOURNAL
DES
SCAVANS,
POUR
L'ANNE'E M. DC LXV.
Par le Sieur DE HEDOUVILLE.
NOUVELLE EDITION.

A PARIS,
Chez PIERRE WITTE, ruë Saint Jacques, vis-à-vis de la
ruë de la Parcheminerie, à l'Ange Gardien.

M. DCCXXIII.
AVEC PRIVILEGE DV ROY.

5   Current Awareness

When books first became the world's main store of knowledge it must have been taken for granted that any newly discovered information, if worth keeping, should be stored in a book. The invention of printing must have reinforced this notion, with a rider added that such new information should be disseminated by means of copies of books. Both the proposition and its rider are still true sometimes, but not always, because they ignore the book's limitations of size. Whereas a book weighs between a few ounces and a few pounds, there are many valuable pieces of information that can be written on less than half an ounce of paper. No one will deny that biography and travel go very well in books, but it is very difficult indeed to write even $\frac{1}{4}$ lb. of new scientific information: most new scientific ideas weigh less than an air-mail letter, and until the 17th century they were communicated between scientists either by mail or not at all.

Denis de Sallo in Paris had the inspiration of becoming a

Although first produced in 1665, the Journal des Sçavans was suppressed for political reasons after only a few issues. It was then produced sporadically until approved in 1723, when a compiled version of all issues up to that date was produced. The frontispiece shown here is of the first edition reissued in that compilation. The journal, in common with the Philosophical Transactions of the Royal Society in London, was one of the first publications to present up-to-date scientific information.

scientific journalist. He informed himself of new scientific equipment and ideas, and wrote accounts of them in his own monthly *Journal des Sçavans*, starting in 1665. This journal became widely read, and soon included papers by originators of new scientific knowledge. Thus authors were no longer encouraged to keep new ideas to themselves until they had enough to fill a book. The secretary of the Royal Society, Henry Oldenburg, began the *Philosophical Transactions*, also in 1665, and other learned societies in Italy, Germany, and the Netherlands followed suit.

Primary Publications

Libraries collected the journals of each society and bound them in volumes containing 50 or more papers, but these were liable to have such a mixture of contents that they would not fit into any but the broadest classification scheme. They could have no proper position on the shelves among single-purpose books, so they were given a place by themselves. Their contents were not in subject order, but in order of date, like bound sets of legal and political reports. They were, however, the primary documents and were liable to be wanted by all sorts of people at any time. More recently, secondary scientific reports, still not long enough to fill a book, summing up the work of three or four closely related primary papers, have appeared in the primary journals. Books, such as textbooks, broad surveys, and encyclopedias, are often tertiary in character.

Developments in duplicating and printing have greatly increased the availability of primary documents. The first practical typewriter was made in Milwaukee, Wisconsin, in 1867; with copying carbons it could be used as a duplicator. The stencil and ink method has many advantages over this, because an ordinary typewriter can be used to prepare a master stencil that will produce 5000 copies. The advent of photography made possible techniques such as blueprints, dyelines, and photostats. Microphotography—a modern version of photocopying—can save time and space. From 100 to 1000 pages can be stored on a single *fiche*, and a chosen page placed at the focus of a viewer in from 5 to 30 seconds.

The very recent development of xerography has brought rapid copying within the reach of people untrained in the technically difficult methods. The xerographic process is electrostatic and demands a fairly complicated but completely automatic machine. Briefly it works like this. A corona discharge produces a uniform electric charge on the machine's selenium plate and a camera throws a positive inverted image of the document onto the plate, discharging it where strong light falls. A fine powder is applied and this sticks to the places that are still charged. A sheet of paper is laid over the plate and another corona discharge transfers the powder from plate to paper. Finally, by heating, the powder is fused permanently onto the paper.

For high-quality, high-volume reproductions of typescript or print, offset processes are available. In these the master is prepared chemically on a metal or paper-like sheet. As each copy is taken, the master is inked and brought into contact with a prepared rubber surface that itself transfers the ink onto the final paper. A new technique has been developed for high-quality typesetting of material directly from magnetic tape. This photocomposition process is controlled by a special-purpose computer. It is already being used to print the *Index Medicus* of the American National Library of Medicine and it could print book catalogs of superb typographic quality very rapidly and at low cost, if made available to libraries at large (see the photographs on page 116).

These more expensive copying devices are used mainly in business offices, but some of their output reaches libraries. The offset method, for instance, is used a great deal for producing technical reports, which may contain similar material to that in journal articles. Technical reports are used internally within large firms and other organizations, and they are on occasion distributed to outsiders. Because of their haphazard distribution, however, they sometimes have the aura of being less authoritative than printed documents, but although they are sometimes hurriedly written, they do provide a quick form of communication between the writer and his often specialist

The photographs on this page show the equipment used in the photo-typesetting of Science Abstracts *and their related indexes and current awareness publications produced by the Institution of Electrical Engineers. Copy is typed on a modified type-writer which produces a paper tape as well as a type-written copy for checking. The paper tape is fed into a computer which stores all information until a particular issue is required. At this point the computer selects the relevant information, sorts it into subject sequence, generates cross-references and indexes, and produces a seven channel magnetic tape (as shown on page 44). The tape is fed into the equipment shown above, which translates the signals into characters on photographic film by producing high speed light flashes through a revolving drum containing negative images of the required symbols. This mechanism is shown in more detail at left (the film magazine is at left of the photograph) and the character drum is shown below, left. The film is used to prepare lithographic plates for conventional offset printing.*

readership. Some are collected by libraries, but they set difficult problems in storage and retrieval.

In many ways, technical reports are suitable for small private
collections, where they are joined by reprints and xerocopies
of articles from journals. Authors of primary or otherwise
important articles in journals receive many requests for copies
of their articles, and the author usually prepares for this
demand by ordering a number of reprints. If supplies fall short,
enquirers can usually make a xerocopy themselves. These
private collections of documents are often small enough to be
arranged in one or two filing cabinets, with a simple alphabetical method of retrieval. They seldom outlast their owner,
because he is the only person who knows the scope of the collection. Unfortunately, libraries cannot depend so much on
human memory, and their documents all need to be indexed
just as elaborately as the articles in the main journals. From
this custodianship of the highly important primary texts, both
loose and in bound form, a new aspect of librarianship has
emerged.

Documentation is a word that has recently enlarged its meaning from the particular to the general, and from a set of objects
to a training. Formerly it meant a special set of documents—
the documentation of an event was a collection of documents
describing that event and others closely connected with it, to
which any historian preparing an account of the event must
continuously refer. This meaning has now been largely superseded, and documentation is one of the arts of a librarian,
mainly in science libraries. It is the management, in a very
broad sense, of the reports and periodicals in the library,
including those that are out on loan or in circulation. These
documents, rather than books, usually comprise the bulk of
scientific collections: for example, 35,000 scientific and technical journals are currently published in the world, carrying
between them nearly 2 million papers or articles per year. In
many journals some (and in some journals all) of the articles
describe the investigation and development of a new and
important idea.

Unfortunately few people read journals from cover to cover

because their contents are so disjointed. Once he has seen the list of contents, glanced at any relevant article and put the journal down, a reader will probably never look at it again; and if he wants to read a particular article again a month or two later he may have difficulty in finding it.

Journals are supposed to be superior to books in one way at least; they are designed to present original material as soon as possible after it is conceived. There are delays, however, in editing and printing, in the queue system, and in the time needed to referee an article. The editors of a journal must collect enough material to fill each number as its date arrives, and they feel safer if they can draw from a small queue of articles. They are helped, and also justified, in building up a queue by the need to ensure that each major article is of the required standard and as original as it claims to be. Even so, journals are the best way of using traditional printing methods to keep a scientist up to date. However, as a glance into any private collection of primary documents will show, they are at present being strongly reinforced by technical reports.

As was mentioned in Chapter 3, scientists discuss their work during visits to laboratories, at conferences, and by correspondence and gossip. Some scientific gatherings are organized by international or national societies, and some are ad hoc affairs in specialist laboratories, but in addition to discussion they also produce numerous papers for publication. It has indeed been formally recognized that each field of science has its own "invisible college" of prestigious researchers who keep each other informed about new results and activities. Although these channels of information do not inform everyone who needs to know, they are nevertheless of great value.

All this is not to decry the important part played by scientific libraries in the information dissemination process, and their main contribution falls into two parts: (1) notifying each individual scientist whenever a new paper appears that is of interest to him—strengthening his current awareness; (2) helping him find earlier papers, which he may or may not have previously seen, about the subject in which he is interested— helping him in retrospective searches.

The drawing at right shows a village
discussion group in progress around
1800. Its modern scientific equivalent
is shown below—a highly organized
conference on nuclear physics,
attended by scientists and technologists from all over the world.
Meetings and discussions are an
integral and very important part of
current awareness, especially for
scientists.

120

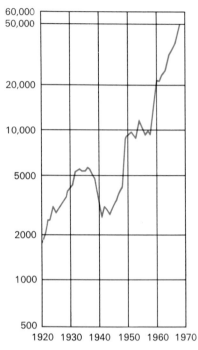

The graph shows the number of abstracts of scientific papers published in Physics Abstracts for the period 1920 to 1968. This and comparable publications provide an essential part of all retrospective services.

Retrospective Services

Statistics are hard to come by, but it is a safe bet that the average scientist or technologist reads at least ten times more current papers than retrospective ones. However, we shall begin by mentioning a very old but still useful device aimed mainly at retrospective work—the publication of separate books of abstracts. These involve an organization of abstractors who systematically read all the literature in a carefully defined field, soon after it is published, and write a short précis of each article. These abstracts, together with the title, author, and journal reference, are classified and published at regular intervals. The user of the abstracts can then gather a great deal of information by scanning through relevant sections of the classified abstracts, and reading those that really concern him. The originators of these valuable publications little realized how the task would grow in magnitude. The graph opposite shows the growth of the world-famous *Physics Abstracts,* published fortnightly in the United Kingdom by the Institution of Electrical Engineers. Over 300 abstractors work at it, and physics societies in many countries have an official interest in its welfare. It has grown from 3000 abstracts per year in the 1940s to 50,000 in the late 1960s. The abstracts are arranged in 23 main chapters divided into 195 subsidiary classes. Besides this vigorous abstracting service there are about a dozen of equivalent standing, each covering a separate section of science and technology, and each prepared by a large panel of experts all qualified to understand the articles in a particular area.

Other, more mechanized, retrospective services offer a wide coverage of less detailed information. For example, the commercially based Institute for Scientific Information, in Philadelphia, stores on magnetic tape the titles, authors, and journal references of over 300,000 articles and other items per year. The annual accumulation of tape is fed into a computer, together with a list of "stop" words such as *the, of, into, a, together, with, such,* and *as,* and a second list of "semi-stop" words such as *monthly* and *fed.* After removing the stop words from the title of each article, the computer makes as many copies of the title as there are keywords in it (that is, words not in the semi-stop list). Each copy is in the same cyclic order, but with a different keyword at the beginning. The entire multiple list is then arranged in alphabetical order and published in four large volumes. There is room for only a bare minimum of information to identify the source of each article and four equally large volumes of adequately detailed source information are also published annually. With the first set an inquirer can easily prepare a suitable list from all the articles having the required keywords in their titles. The second set gives a full reference to the journal in which the article appeared.

A similar service of the Institute uses the citation indexing system discussed in the previous chapter. However, remember that someone relying entirely on such retrospective services would be reading articles two years and more after their original publication.

Current Awareness

We therefore come to the question of preparing publications that will strengthen the scientist's current awareness, by bringing articles to his notice within a few months of publication. The Physics Abstracts organization, for example, publishes twice monthly *Current Papers in Physics*, a classified list of 60 classes of newly published articles whose abstracts appear in *Physics Abstracts*. The subscriber to *Current Papers in Physics* receives his information one to three months after the article's first publication. The Institute for Scientific Information gives a speedier service, with an average of only 18 days delay. Its *Current Contents to Space, Electronic and Physical Sciences* is a bound set of photocopies of the contents pages of 600 journals each week together with an index of authors and their addresses but no classification. Some of the contents pages appear simultaneously with the original journals as a result of an arrangement whereby some publishers send proof copies of contents pages before publication. By making available to scientific staff the appropriate index, abstract, and current-awareness publications, local libraries can play a very large part in this type of information service, though before long their role will probably be taken over by very large computer centers.

Selective Dissemination of Information

Local libraries now, and computer centers in the future, can greatly assist the current awareness of scientists by what is known as Selective Dissemination of Information, or SDI. There is no mystery about SDI, for it uses exactly the same tools and techniques that are used in retrospective searching, but they are applied to all documents immediately after they first enter the library. The aim is to present each individual scientist with a list of new titles whittled down to only those articles that really interest him. When the unwanted material has been successfully weeded out, a short summary of the article can be included with each title (many journals insist that each of their articles begins with a short summary). In the last resort, of course, when the system is so accurate that all the articles it selects are of real interest, a facsimile of the entire article might as well be included there and then.

SDI is equally helpful to small, closely knit groups of people as well as to individuals. The group or individual has a "profile," a copy of which is kept by the librarian or the computer. The profile describes the user's information needs, and it is carefully prepared for matching with the description of each document that comes into the library. We have already seen that there are many ways of systematically describing documents, ranging from the UDC system, through keywords in titles, to special sets of descriptors. Any of these systems can be used as long as the user's profile is expressed in the language of the description system operating in the library. Thus a profile should be identical with the description of a hypothetical article describing the whole of a group's work. Should such an article turn up on the librarian's desk he would be fully satisfied that the group needed it and would notify them without hesitation. However, the librarian is far more likely to see an article with quite a lot in common with some aspects of the group's work. The profile and the article's description would then not match perfectly, but overlap appreciably. The librarian has to use his judgment or, more likely, apply a few rules before deciding whether or not to notify the group.

Unfortunately librarians are busy people, and soon run into difficulties when they try to serve more than two or three users in this way. Without mechanical aids they understandably prefer to cut out all use of special descriptor languages for profiles and documents, and make a short cut to the final decision. No doubt this heuristic method works very well for serving the board of directors and a few other favored people, but when every member of a large organization clamors for SDI there are invariably too few librarians available to cope.

In these circumstances either there is a restricted service or SDI becomes completely mechanical. In our present epoch of growth, however, managements deciding to adopt a computer-based SDI system are taking the plunge indeed. They commit themselves to years of preparatory work, including system design, purchase of hardware and programs, and massive preparation of data. They run a risk that the staff may not find the system beneficial when it arrives, but this is only a slight risk. The far larger risk they run is that their system will be out of date soon, if not before it is implemented. At the time of writing the most imminent development appears to be a central computer with a complete store of current awareness data, punched in by a large and well-organized staff, and connected by means of a public data communication network (similar in many ways to the telephone system) to subscribers located hundreds or even thousands of miles away, at less cost than any worthwhile do-it-yourself system.

I can imagine going into my office in the middle 1970s— hardly have I sat down at my desk when an electropneumatic conveyor delivers my telex correspondence and other material from the computer terminal in our building. The ordinary mail has already been received at the central registry but will not reach me until much later in the morning. I put some correspondence aside for direct reply, and send other items to our local registry with requests for the relevant previous correspondence. Then I pick up a long strip of paper folded like a concertina into five or six pages. Each page except the second is blank (for technical reasons) except for two or three lines of cryptic type. The top page tells the conveyor controls my room number, and contains my name, the date, and time of dispatch. The second page is a list of numbers, which the computer will decode only on request, representing the journals that have been examined at the computer center in the last 24 hours. Each of the subsequent pages contains particulars of one paper from one of these journals, whose descriptor statement matches enough of my profile statement to satisfy a chosen set of rules for matching. The first paper seems to be about the preparation of descriptor sets. Another is by a very belligerent author whose views I always find stimulating. A third is about the application of graph theory to a problem of pattern recognition. The others are not of much interest, so I keypunch a minute to the librarian asking to see the first and third as soon as possible and have my name put on a waiting list for the second. Ten minutes after picking up the concertina I can put it away in a drawer and get on with some other task. The work leading to my concertina of information included a great deal of keypunching in various data preparation rooms in South Wales, some reels of magnetic tape received in Manchester by airmail from Washington, overnight processing of all this data by a large computer in Manchester, and a message transmitted over the national data network at about 6 A.M. to the data terminal in my building—and, of course, the work of the authors and publishers of the articles selected for me to consider.

The above dream is realizable now, but it is overoptimistic to expect it to happen so quickly in the United Kingdom. It is, however, a reasonable prophecy for the United States, which in computer developments is about five years ahead of the rest of the world. It is unlikely to come true in Europe until the late 1970s. Therefore we must examine the state of SDI as it now stands in America. It was recently summarized, with a bias toward physics, by six members of the staff of the American Institute of Physics, in *Annual Review of Information Science and Technology*, Vol. 2, p. 339, 1967, with the title "Techniques for Publication and Distribution of Information." They mentioned four firms and six government agencies that had made achievements already by 1967, and one firm and one university that were then well on the way. Among the firms were a famous maker of computers and indefatigable developers of their applications, together with leading chemical, communications, and aircraft corporations. The government agencies included the United States Atomic Energy Commission and the National Aeronautics and Space Administration. These are all huge concerns operating in several different fields, and a private SDI system can be expected to flourish in each of them; the world must wait until they report on their achievements and trends. The ideal, though, would be a worldwide public system. The Institution of Electrical Engineers, which already produces journals of abstracts for world consumption, is preparing the structure of such a public system.

The pioneers, who are thus risking capital and prestige while hoping to improve the efficiency of their organizations, will undoubtedly lead us in time to a sound understanding of information retrieval, at least in technological literature. The evaluation of their systems will happen naturally—the proof of the pudding will be in the eating—but information scientists are unanimous in the pessimistic view that it will be a long and tiresome job.

One helpful way to speed the process and reduce the indigestion is by parallel, more academic approaches (it goes on all the time). All conceivable aspects of the problem are separately investigated, models are made, and pilot experiments are conducted, with the intention that practical experiences of information retrieval shall have the best theoretical support. The National Science Foundation in 1966, with its 14th volume on *Current Research and Development in Scientific Documentation*, listed 655 such projects and gave a brief account of each of them. (The NSF in Washington is to be congratulated on this compilation. Although a year or more behind at the time of publication, it genuinely improves current awareness, and it is studied especially by the research workers, who send in to it descriptions of their work on documentation.) To provide an overall picture of this activity is far beyond the descriptive powers of this book, but the NSF has been able to classify documentation research into the following nine main classes. (1) Information needs and uses (behavioral studies of users; citation studies; communication patterns; literature use studies). (2) Document creation and copying (computer-assisted compositions; microforms; recording and storing; writing and editing). (3) Language analysis (computational linguistics; lexicography; natural language text processing; psycholinguistics; semantic analysis). (4) Translation (machine translation; translation aids). (5) Abstracting, classification, coding, and indexing (classification and indexing systems; content analysis; machine-aided classification, extracting, and indexing; vocabulary studies). (6) System design (information centers; information retrieval; mechanization of library operations; selective dissemination of information). (7) Analysis and evaluation (comparative studies; indexing quality; modeling; test methods and performance measures; translation quality). (8) Pattern re-cognition (image processing; speech analysis). (9) Adaptive systems (artificial intelligence; automata; problem solving; self-organizing systems).

The work entailed in these projects is shown by the follow-ing quotations, one from a project in class 6, and one from class 7. Project number 6.17 has as its objective, "To study possible uses of computers in connection with the project of a 'General Inventory of Monuments and Works of Art' located in France, under the Ministry of Cultural Affairs. Among the proposed uses are: (a) mechanical retrieval on specific search topics, (b) mechanical preparation of printed catalogs and indexes, and (c) automatic classification." Project number 7.15 in Indianapolis is, "To compare different methods of input to an organic chemical structure retrieval system for a file of 100,000 compounds." The diagram on page 128 shows a fairly simple example of how an organic molecule can be rep-resented in four ways, the last two suitable for input to a com-puter store. Chemists are concerned about such things as finding whether a molecule is new or not, listing all the molecules con-taining a particular substructure, and finding the nearest molecule to any given molecule, possibly with a view to manu-facturing one from the other. All these turn out to be exception-ally difficult problems, which for large molecules go beyond the powers of even our biggest computers.

Another NSF publication—*Nonconventional Scientific and Technical Information Systems in Current Use*, No. 4, 1966—gives details of 175 systems. The two with the largest number of documents are the American Cyanamid Co. and the Armed Forces Institute of Pathology, each with over 7 million documents by 1966. Both use computers, and produce query services in the form of retrospective searches. The smallest number of documents is at the Survey Research Center of the University of California, at Berkeley. In three years this center has added only 50 documents per year to its collection of demographic surveys in Asia, Latin America, and Africa, but each document was transferred in detail to a computer at a cost of $1000 each.

3-carbamoyl-1, 2-diazabicyclo [3.1.0] hexane

Four different representations of one chemical molecule are shown at left. (1) The full chemical name. (2) A structural diagram of the molecule (with numbers 1–9 for reference in the table). (3) The Wiswesser notation. (4) A connection table for the molecule. Both (3) and (4) are topological descriptions suitable for encoding into a computer. They enable rapid checking in a register to ensure that no molecule has been entered twice or that no two molecules are sharing one entry, and also permit comparison to be made between molecules to find which parts of their structures are similar.

T35 AN FMTJ EVZ

Node no.	Node value	Bond to	Bond valve
1	C	—	—
2	C	1	1
3	N	1	1
4	C	1	1
5	C	2	1
6	N	3	1
7	O	4	2
8	N	4	1
9	C	5	1

Ring closure	Bond value
5-6	1
6-9	1

Evaluation of Retrieval Systems

Even from the few examples quoted, it is clear that document collections and retrieval systems and experiments differ enormously in type and purpose. Why are we, along with the NSF and the readers of their publications, so interested in what they are all doing? The chief answer is, because we want to know how successful they are, how worth while. Most of the non-conventional systems in current use depend for their evaluation on reports or answers to questionnaires by their users. Comparisons of systems are difficult on this basis, though of course, for operating systems, the satisfaction of the clientele is the main thing.

The evaluation of all retrieval systems on the same basis would be achieved if we could apply either of two techniques that have been well proven in dealing with standard measurements in physics, such as frequency, mass, length, and temperature. The first of these would require a standard set of documents, with a set of inquiries for which the optimum response is known, to be processed by each retrieval system to be evaluated. There is no hope of using this method, because every retrieval system is designed for a particular field of documents and inquiries; and no set of documents and inquiries can be devised that would be a fair test for all. The second technique is not applicable either, for it would have to be based on a master information retrieval system equally capable of handling documents and inquiries in any field; and no such master system exists.

When these essentially practical approaches fail it is often worth while to turn to mathematical theory, and examine whether there exists a more fundamental way of handling the problem in some of its elementary forms. If there is, then perhaps real cases may be compared with the abstractions that mathematics can handle; possibly the difference between two actual retrieval systems will be similar to the difference between two related abstractions. One would expect that, in making a mathematical theory about information retrieval, a good starting point would be the mathematics of information that Shannon originated, briefly considered in Chapter 1. The vast literature on information retrieval shows little evidence of this having been done, and this omission is probably due to a common misconception about the two "informations."

The information of Shannon, which he equated with the statistical concept of entropy, is measured from the statistics of the signals used in any given form of communication. The information obtained by reading a book is some kind of interaction between the records already in the brain and the new material as it is put in; intangible and subjective, it is totally unlike that of Shannon. With which of the two is information retrieval concerned? Because it involves books, the facile answer is the mental information, but is not this a mistake?

In an ordinary retrieval situation, what is the "information" that is retrieved? We have seen that it is a list of the names, numbers, or addresses of documents in a given collection. Nothing more will happen until the inquirer starts to read in the expectation that a fair proportion of the documents so described will turn out to be relevant to his inquiry. The mental information does not flow until some time after the information of Shannon's type has been retrieved. Let us suppose there are N documents in the collection, and they are identified by the numbers 1 to N. The retrieval system, as we have seen, contains certain particulars of each document, and it has a method of matching any inquiry with each document in turn and listing the documents that appear to match. Thus the input to the system is an inquiry, and its output is a list of numbers, all between 1 and N.

What would the ideal output be if the inquirer was told exactly what he wanted to know? It would be a list of numbers, representing all the documents that the inquirer would consider relevant but leaving out all irrelevant documents. The ideal list is information, and it is measurable by Shannon's method. In measuring it, we shall find there are two contributions to the total information: the larger contribution (usually) comes from the list of relevant documents itself, but another contribution—smaller though not negligible— comes from the implicit list of all the documents that have not been chosen. The same total information can be represented by a string of N 0's and 1's in strict order, and this representation shows very well the connection with information theory. In the following example $N = 50$, and this notation has been used to write down the "messages" of the actual and the ideal retrieval exercises, in an imaginary case, of course:

Ideal   00000 01000 00000 00000 00100 10000 00000 00000 00000 00000

Actual   00000 01000 00000 00001 00000 10000 00000 00000 00100 00000

The example represents the ideal and actual response to some inquiry made at a library containing 50 documents. Documents 7 and 26 are included in both the ideal and the actual response. Numbers 20 and 43 were actually retrieved but were irrelevant. Number 23 should have been retrieved but was not.

To a communications engineer the two strings of 0's and 1's would look like a message put into a communication channel and the resulting message received at the other end. The message received is not the same as the message sent, so he would call it a "noisy" communication channel. It is as if the library tried to give the correct answer to the inquirer but the message got partly confused on the way.

Shannon gave a mathematical formula for calculating the amount of information in a message received through a noisy communication channel. It is a little more complicated than the formula in Chapter 1, which is for a noise-free channel, but it can easily be applied. When the message is a sequence using only 2 symbols (0 and 1 in our case) there are 4 contributions to the total information—this is equal to the square of the number of symbols. We shall modify the above example, making it a little more realistic, by taking a library of 1000 documents. As before, 3 documents ought to have been retrieved; only 2 of them were retrieved, together with 2 others that were irrelevant. Shannon's formula, applied to information retrieval, can be written (the logarithms are to the base 2)

$$I = A \log NA/(A+B)(A+C) + B \log NB/(A+B)(B+D) + \\ C \log NC/(A+C)(C+D) + D \log ND/(B+D)(C+D)$$

The letters A, B, C, D, should be derived from statistical probabilities multiplied by N, but for the present example it is reasonable to take them as actual counts of documents, as shown below:

	Relevant	Irrelevant
Retrieved	$A = 2$	$B = 2$
Not retrieved	$C = 1$	$D = 995$

$(N = A+B+C+D = 1000)$

Applying this formula the four contributions to the total information are:

from the 2 correct documents retrieved	14.7 bits
from the 995 incorrect documents not retrieved	2.9 bits
from the 2 incorrect documents retrieved	—2.0 bits
from the 1 correct document not retrieved	—1.6 bits
	total 14.0 bits

The total of 14.0 bits is a substantial amount of information.

If just the 3 correct documents had been retrieved, the information would have been 29.6 bits.

Calculations like this could be made for real cases, with one reservation that will be discussed later. No doubt there are many considerations that make 14.0 bits out of a possible 29.6 rather an unrealistic account of the imperfections or the validity of a retrieval system. The inquirer may not at all mind having to look at 2 extra documents only to find them irrelevant. He may be furious at being given only 2 relevant documents when he should have had 3; or, on the other hand, he may be so pleased with the first of his 2 relevant documents that he does not want to use anything else. None of these objections seems powerful enough to make the information-theory approach a nonstarter, and yet there is no evidence that it has ever been given a serious trial. I have written a short paper on this subject, which has been accepted by the international journal *Information Storage and Retrieval*.

In practice, to the accompaniment of much controversy and discussion, various statistical measurements have been devised, and they are often useful at the experimental or design stage of a retrieval system. They are nearly all variations on a pair of measurements called *recall factor* and *pertinency factor*. The recall factor of any particular search, by hand or by machine, is the ratio between the number of relevant documents that were retrieved and the number that ought to have been retrieved $(A/A+C)$. The average value of this ratio, when it has been measured from a large and representative set of searches in a particular library by a particular system, is the recall factor of that system.

It is perhaps easier to consider one search rather than an overall average. Two comments arise immediately. First, how are we to count, in a practical case, all the documents that ought to have been retrieved? To do so, we should have to know the document collection very well indeed, or some deus ex machina would have to perform a special search on our behalf. This difficulty effectively rules out the measurement of recall factor in working libraries. For experimental systems where retrieval ideas are being tested, there is no choice but to know the document collection very thoroughly. Some collections are kept very small for this reason, with perhaps only 200 documents, and then it is not always easy to show that they are truly representative of any practical collection with real retrieval problems. Others, with perhaps 10,000 documents, limit their test inquiries, applying them over and over again with different search and classification strategies, until enough knowledge has accumulated for a fairly complete list of documents relevant to each inquiry to be compiled. In this case, it has to be shown that the limited number of perhaps 100 test inquiries is truly representative of the inquiries likely to be made in a real situation. The second comment on recall factor is that it ignores all the documents that the inquirer looks at but rejects as being irrelevant. Clearly the best possible value of a recall factor is 1.0, when the number of relevant documents retrieved is equal to the number that ought to be retrieved.

It hardly takes a genius to discover that there is a simple way to produce a recall factor of 1.0 in answer to every inquiry: hand the client the whole collection of documents! And this is where the pertinency factor comes in: it is the ratio between the number of relevant documents retrieved in a search and the total number retrieved ($A/A + B$). When the whole collection of documents is retrieved the pertinency factor is almost bound to be small. It would be 1.0 if only a few documents were retrieved and they were all relevant, but then, probably, a number of other relevant documents would still lie buried in the collection and the recall factor would be rather small. In fact, as the pertinency factor goes up, the recall factor goes down, and vice versa. The graph on page 134, taken from a report by C. H. Cleverdon, illustrates the kind of relation between the two factors.

If libraries knew nothing about the requirements of their customers, and had to choose between alternative retrieval systems, they would probably consider first the system for which the product of the recall and pertinency factors (averaged over a large number of test inquiries) was the largest. In this way they would get the best of both worlds. In effect, they would be using a single factor (it has not so far been named to uni-

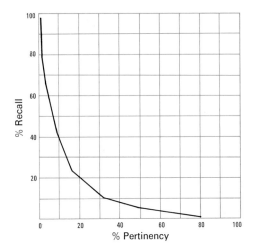

The graph shows the performance of the best of a series of experimental index languages in a test of 42 questions on a collection of 1400 documents. The relationship between recall and pertinency (both defined in the text) produces a hyperbolic curve.

versal satisfaction) whose value is $A^2/(A + B)(A + C)$—that is, (number of relevant documents retrieved)^2/(number of documents retrieved) × (total number of relevant documents in collection). This factor is often used as one of the measures of success in experimental work.

However, libraries usually cater for one of two sorts of customer. As we have seen, a patent classification system has to be so meticulous that inquirers can be almost certain of finding a previous relevant patent if one exists—here the recall factor must be very large, well above 0.9. On the other hand researchers for information like our simple Belshazzar example are satisfied to find a single document with the answer in it, although many other documents may also have the answer. For them the library naturally tries to cut down the fruitless reading of unhelpful documents, and so the pertinency factor should be reasonably large, and near 1.0 if possible. Librarians have known all about this dichotomy for many years and they would probably prefer to use their own nomenclature, calling patent searching a "generic survey" and Belshazzar a "specific reference." There is no harm at all in librarians and experimentalists having these two points of view, if they continue to cooperate for the benefit of their clientele.

We may seem to have wandered a long way from selective dissemination of information and the technologist's need for current awareness, but this is only an illusion. What is good for retrospective searching is also good for the improvement of current awareness. Although, for convenience, ideas and systems are tried out on a basic collection rather than a growing one, a good method of putting one's finger on a piece of information that entered the library 1 to 10 years ago will also enable a relevant piece of information to be found that entered the library last week.

Perhaps we have used the word *library* a little too freely. Sir Frank Francis, as Director and Principal Librarian of the British Museum, referred to the library as "a healing place of the soul," but he went on to quote J. W. Clark, an expert on the medieval library, as saying in 1894, "A library may be considered from two very different points of view: as a workshop or as a museum . . . the former commends itself to the practical turn of mind characteristic of the present day; common sense urges that mechanical ingenuity, which has done so much in other directions, should be employed in making the acquisition of knowledge less cumbrous and less tedious." Sixty years later, in a set of recommendations to the technical community, the Weinberg report asked for specialized information centers and central depositories as described on page 77 of Chapter 3.

These things are for the immediate future, and indeed they are happening now. However, the next chapter looks further ahead, toward the year 2000. By then the specialized information center will be even less like the libraries of today. Paradoxically, it will be much more like a very wise librarian.

6 On-line

Progress from the early beginnings to the conversational method of using computers has been remarkably swift, and it is difficult to find anything like it in history, with the possible exception of certain weapons of war. For over a decade people have been able to buy the time of large computers for prices around $100 per minute. It is up to the customers to decide whether it is profitable to pay this price in return for the services provided—and more and more of them are finding that it is. Thus the services of computers are treated just like any other commodity, from electric power and iron ore at one end of the scale to the services of office cleaners, advertising agents, and management consultants at the other. Computers have had nothing directly to offer librarians, however, except for a rather limited choice of indirect services such as the KWIC index, the citation index, and some Selective Dissemination of Information. The library information that has so far been put into computer stores has been restricted more or less to titles,

Multiaccess computers that can accept requests from many sources and process them sequentially at very high speed without confusion are now being used in situations where rapid retrieval of information is vital. In the air terminal shown opposite, cathode-ray tube display units are used to present information from a central computer about services and seat availability. Seats can be reserved and bookings confirmed in a matter of seconds.

authors, and reference particulars of articles in scientific and technical periodicals.

The reasons for this are not hard to find. First, library information is very expensive to put into computer stores, simply because it is so bulky. Second, not nearly enough experience has been gained of classification systems to guarantee a reasonable return for the effort of putting indexed information into a computer store before the classification system becomes obsolete. The third reason is bound up with the second, and that is the rather limited use that could have been made of stored indexed information even if it had been available. In this chapter we shall discuss a revolution in computer usage that will make the third reason, at any rate, null and void.

Until very recently the only available services of commercial computers were akin to those of a laundry or a typing bureau. The work was sent off, and in the fullness of time it came back in the required form. There was, and still is, plenty of computer work for which a time delay of hours or days is perfectly acceptable. Anything that had to be answered immediately had to be done by some other method. Even if a firm owned a complete computer to itself the computing work was usually done in batches—wages slips were prepared weekly, stock lists and stock movements every day, and so on. However, when people have a computer of their own they can, if they wish, sit down at its console and manipulate the controls even while their ideas of what they want to do are only partly formed. Conceivably, if these people are exceptionally clever, they may for example produce a new program more quickly this way than by writing it at a desk.

Only computers of certain designs are suitable for this approach and the earliest electronic computers, such as the ACE at the National Physical Laboratory, in the United Kingdom, were often used like this. The ACE, for instance, did the bulk of its real *work* by assimilating batches of cards (of two types, called *programs* and *data*) and by punching out other batches of cards (called *results*) that were interpreted by card-reading machines. However the ACE spent a good deal of its *time* with a user sitting at the console (see photo on page

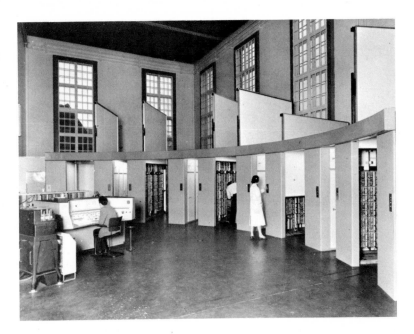

The photograph above shows the ACE digital computer, designed and built at the National Physical Laboratory, in operation. This computer was particularly useful for teaching programming because the information in the stores could be displayed on cathode-ray screens and any part of a program altered by use of keys and switches on the console. This conversational facility also allowed programs to be composed on-line.

139) testing his program and getting it into perfect form for operation. The user would frequently manipulate switches and examine the rows of lights and cathode-ray screens showing the contents of the working stores of ACE. He would, for example, make the machine run through parts of the program one instruction at a time and would check the stores contents to see that the desired changes took place for each instruction. He could even make a setting of keys to produce the same effect as an instruction from a card-punched program, check the result, and if the move was successful, make the computer put it on a card later.

Although he would not have used the expression in those days, he was having a conversation with ACE in a low-level language. He was giving meaningful signals to ACE via the keys and switches and receiving other signals back immediately via the displays. Any spectator was, of course, completely mystified unless he knew how to interpret both the signals in and the signals out. They were in machine language, but even the uninstructed onlooker could see that signals were flowing both to and from the machine. He no doubt thought of them as trial and response, whereas it would be easier today to think of them as question and answer.

A few of the more brilliant members of the NPL learned to operate ACE without any formal instruction except a rather sketchy loose-leaf operation manual and a run-through of what the switches and display screens did. They would sit at the console late at night, to avoid interrupting other people's work, and converse with the machine until they found which instructions it would obey in the desired manner—in other words the machine taught the user its language. The process was closely allied to the way students in modern language laboratories learn from a machine the structure of foreign languages. However, ACE was a teaching machine not only for the brilliant few, but for all its programmers. Whenever it stopped in the course of a faulty program, the operator could examine the contents of each store in turn, or he could have a postmortem card output of the contents of all stores. By studying this information he could find where his program was wrong.

High-level Language and On-line Programming

Most people who programmed the early computers will admit nostalgia for the times when they had virtually to work out, detail by detail, the internal states of their machine as it progressed through their program. Without doubt their task was intellectually satisfying, and of great service to the community, but it tended to become repetitive. At first these pioneers developed personal short cuts, in the form of private subroutines—sections of program that they used repeatedly in many main programs. Some became valuable enough to be put into a subroutine library for general use. But there was an obvious need to examine systematically the technique of program writing, and cut out as much repetitive thinking and writing as possible. If tedious tasks were unavoidable by direct

methods, many of them could be transferred to the computer—
at some cost in computer time, but with an overall saving.

Efforts in this direction produced a surprising result as they
matured. The new programs were seen to have some of the
grammatical properties of spoken language—words in several
grammatical classes, and syntax. This was the time when the
expression "programming language" caught on, and a
language capable of succinctly instructing a computer to carry
out varied and complicated tasks earned the epithet "high-
level."

In the late 1950s research workers were developing high-
level languages such as Autocode, Fortran, and Algol, designed
to save time and thinking effort in programming. In general,
single easily memorized instructions were transferred to paper
tape or cards using a keypunching typewriter and thence to a
computer. With the help of a *compiler* program already stored
in the computer, these were automatically converted into a
sequence of machine instructions. For example an instruction
in typewriter code such as PRINT "THE ANSWER IS"
SQR(B—A) + C would be converted within the computer
to a sequence containing dozens of instructions. Its effect
would be that the typewritten output from the machine would
read THE ANSWER IS .870766 (or whatever $\sqrt{B—A} + C$
came to, when the stored values of A, B, and C were inserted).
Just as in low-level codes, the programmer had to be meticulous
over everything he typed. If he had omitted the quotation
marks before THE, the machine would have looked among
its stores for one labeled THE and, finding none, would have
prepared a message "Failure type 284 in line 122" or perhaps
"Undefined variable in line 122" and then stopped working.
On receiving this message some time later, the programmer
would have to look at line 122 of his typed version of the program (containing the offending THE), find what was wrong
with it, and send a correction message, instructing the computer to modify its stored but uncompiled version of the
program, and try again.

The first few months in the life of a program would usually
be spent in being debugged and in having its algorithm per-

142

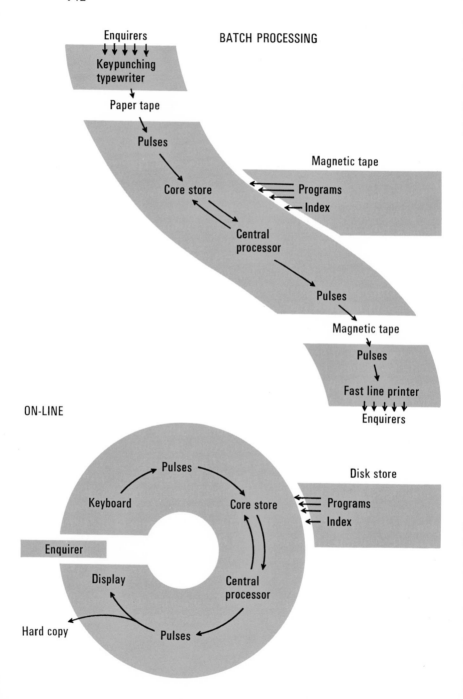

fected, and the above example is a very simple case of debugging where a high-level language is used. In these early stages the program usually goes into the computer twice: first to be compiled, and then in binary form to be run. (Later, only the binary form will be used.) To make efficient use of the computer's time, a number of programs have to be compiled in a batch (the compiler program having been written into the computer's core store), and perhaps half an hour later the batch of binary versions are written at one time into the core store and run consecutively.

The messages from a computer about errors in high-level programs are carefully worked out in the beginning by the writers of the compiler program. If they wished, they could have included a set of instructions for the computer to run through a series of extra tests whenever it came across a cause of failure like an undefined variable, and one of the tests might be, for instance, to check that the characters following the set of characters PRINT included an even number of quotation marks. Then a more precise failure report could be sent. Compiler programs are such large and complex programs that their writers have to draw the line somewhere, and for batch processing it is better to give the programmer a rough idea about several errors than a precise indication of one.

High-level languages invariably require costly compiler programs and these take up much of the computer's core store while they are in use, though they may be removed when the computer is not needed for compiling. A second limitation is that the compiled program is never as efficient as it could be if written directly in a low-level code, and consequently requires longer than the minimum time to run. However, the run-time of a high proportion of programs is extremely short, perhaps even less than a second. The advantage of high-level languages is, of course, that they greatly reduce the program writing time. It can confidently be said that, but for high-level languages, a

The diagrams shown opposite compare batch processing and on-line methods used for information retrieval. In the batch-processing system the enquirers must state the quantity of output they require (number of titles etc) before the process is started. Each batch is likely to contain several hundred requests although batch size is regulated to economize on movement of magnetic tape (on reels) storing programs and index. Retrieval of the desired information from the on-line display unit will probably involve several circuits of the diagram as the enquirer narrows down his choice from a wide range of material.

very great number of programs now available, especially for advanced applications of computers, would still be waiting to be written.

After the first flush of early computers came a series of models particularly suitable for commercial use, designed to be used chiefly by firms who required only a few programs but who had large quantities of data to process. As a result the ability to sit at a console and test new programs was lost. Instead, they had to be sent for batch processing, and this was a handicap for research workers and learners. Although the development of high-level languages did not itself remove this handicap, we shall see that it was a step in the right direction because it improved the speed of comprehension and utterance at the human end of man-machine communication.

The difficulty caused by the need for batching was first circumvented by a few teaching institutions, in particular Dartmouth College, New Hampshire. They acquired a small secondhand computer and designed a high-level language, called BASIC, especially for teaching. It was quite limited in its scope, compared with Algol and Fortran, but it specialized in the clarity and comprehensiveness of its error messages. For instance the error about "THE," already discussed, would cause the computer to reply "line 122: store labeled THE not found." Thus if computer time was available for a student to sit at the typewriter in direct communication with the computer, he could correct his program straight away, by typing in the correct version of line 122.

In this way the student had the same facility as the early ACE programmers, checking and amending his program while on-line with the computer. Much more than that, he had the advantage of an easy high-level language. Instead of laboriously inserting instructions a single binary digit at a time, he typed a few words, and a compiler program already stored in the computer converted them into the binary code it needed, and put them into a different store reserved for the compiled program. Without further ado the computer then proceeded to follow the instructions in the compiled program. Students were able to learn the fundamentals of computer operation in a few weeks, and to write quite sophisticated programs—usually involving mathematical operations on a small amount of data. When one calculation had been made and the answers printed out, the data could easily be replaced by fresh data and the same calculation performed on these.

Here, as an example, is an imaginary conversation between a programmer (working for a firm whose code number is 11009) and a computer. The comments in small type are not part of the conversation.

ON AT 12:02 LNDN 23/10/69	typed by computer when telephone call made
USER NUMBER— 11009	the service will be charged to this account
SYSTEM— BASIC	program will be written in BASIC
NEW OR OLD— NEW	program is not already stored in computer's files
NEW FILE NAME— RENO	this name will recall program if it is stored
READY	a store has been reserved and named RENO
10 FOR I = 1 TO 5	do it 5 times
20 PRINT INT (6 RND(X) + 1),	RND(X): select a number at random between 0 and 1 to 6 places of decimals. 6 RND(X) is a number between 0.000000 and 5.999999. 6 RND (X)+1 is a number between 1.000000 and 6.999999. INT: omit all figures after the decimal point; so INT (6 RND(X) +1) is a whole number between 1 and 6 inclusive
RUN	compile program and run it

ILLEGAL FORMULA IN LINE 20   multiplication sign * needed between 6 and RND

FOR WITHOUT NEXT   the instruction NEXT is necessary to return action to line 10

20 PRINT INT (6*RND(X) + 1),

30 NEXT I

RUN

RENO   LNDN 11009   12:10   23/10/69

6   6   1   3   2   all whole numbers at random between 1 and 6

RAN   0.22 SEC.   central computer occupied for 0.22 seconds

READY   programmer could now type RUN and have 5 more random numbers

LIST   type whole program as it stands

RENO   LNDN 11009   12:13   23/10/69

10 FOR I = 1 TO 5

20 PRINT INT (6*RND(X) + 1),

30 NEXT I

SAVE   keep program in store

READY   it is now in store

BYE   action finished

***OFF AT 12:15 ELAPSED TERMINAL TIME = 13 MIN.
    computer now terminates the telephone call

The above is a shortened version of a conversation that results in a program to choose five numbers at random, between 1 and 6. It would obviously be very convenient for playing poker dice without dice. The instructions RND and INT happen to be available in this language because they are often useful in more serious programs: in their absence, a more elaborate program would have been necessary. In this example it has not been possible to explore many of the powers of BASIC, which in its turn is much less powerful than some other high-level languages, and the program itself is untypically short in comparison with the routine conversation before and after it.

When the time comes to invite an inquirer to converse with a computer, not merely about a program or a relatively small amount of data, but about a huge store of library information, what differences will there be? We have seen that no system providing such a facility yet exists for general use, but that the necessary equipment and technical knowledge are available. Quite large computerized stores of library information are already being assembled, notably in the fields of law, medicine, and chemistry, and though initially access to them will be by batch processing methods, they will be available for conversational access when the time comes. There still remains the task of designing and testing a system that will make such conversation possible and effective. Other tasks of higher priority, such as medical uses of computers in hospitals, are occupying all the available technical effort, and the numerous but rather small groups researching on information retrieval are busy gathering basic experience that will make future design decisions easier and more satisfactory.

Input and Output Equipment

The choice of equipment for such a project can be made at any time, however, assuming that the choice lies among the equipment available now. There is no particular difficulty about choosing the computers and information stores, but the question of what type of input and output terminals to use is worth considering. The on-line typewriter used by students for learning about programming is hardly good enough, even if it can be designed to be silent in operation. It is tedious to use, for both input and output messages. The inquirer will not like having to type a series of error-free

The photograph above shows input and output equipment being used on-line to a computer during a research project at the National Physical Laboratory. A graph of word associations is being displayed direct from the computer store (seen in the background). The points represent words, the lines are associations. The typewriter is used for communication either way between the operator and the computer. The light pen at the side of the screen can be used to alter parts of the displayed figure. The display unit at left is being used for computer-aided design. The advantages of such presentation are that the effects of alteration in specifications can be seen immediately by the designer.

messages, or to wait while fairly long replies are typed out at only a few hundred words a minute.

One way around the difficulty is to use fast line printers for the computer's replies, but these are large and costly machines. They are not the sort of equipment to install at simple inquiry terminals, because they will be idle for a large part of the time, while the inquirer reads the message and thinks what to do next. It would therefore be advisable to look for something else, something compact and quiet to operate, and suitable for a number of inquirers to use in the same room, possibly, each at his own outfit.

As things now stand, the most attractive "something else" is the *display*—an apparatus that comprises a set of hardware, and programs stored in a computer, controlling a cathode-ray tube at the user's desk. The display has several radically different uses, but for our case up to about 100 words can be presented at a time on the cathode-ray screen. The computer can prepare the necessary signals for such a small number of words in seconds, and the operator-inquirer can read them through in about a minute. If he wishes, he can press a button and order a "hard copy" to be prepared for him to take away—this may not be ready at once, because it requires what amounts to a piece of batch processing. The words he has copied and reads on the screen might be an abstract of a document, or references to a document, or verbal and numerical information to help the inquirer formulate his next message to the computer.

But how is he to deliver his message? The choices are: (1) to use a teletypewriter in addition to the display; (2) to use a typewriter keyboard to set up instructions on the cathode-ray screen (in the high-level language of the computer) and then press a key to dispatch the message to the computer; or (3) to have the computer present on the screen a choice of messages that he might wish to send, from which he can select one. This variety of messages can be increased enormously if the computer choices are presented stage by stage in hierarchical form, just like a hierarchical classification system.

The third alternative was chosen by the System Development Corporation at Santa Monica, California, for their project called **BOLD** (Bibliographic On-line Library Display), which uses at each inquiry station a teletypewriter, on which any of a list of comments (usually single words) can be typed by the operator, and a cathode-ray screen with a light pen (see later). It is as yet only a prototype, but it is intended for later development as a large-scale computer-based document storage and retrieval system. The software part of the display subsystem is stored in the central computer. The BOLD system has three principal functions: (a) to allow browsing through a magnetic tape file, arranged linearly like a library shelf, and displaying the titles, authors, and abstracts of documents in the sequence in which they have been classified; (b) to provide a capability for requesting documents on a given subject by combining index terms—the user may select the relevant documents from a display of document references and abstracts; and (c) to permit the study of the comparative retrieval effectiveness of various indexing and classification systems.

But is all well with available methods of requesting documents with an on-line retrieval system? Ideally, the user would like to treat the computer just like a librarian, and send it any message, in any form of words that occur to him. If the computer is equipped to classify documents put into it in natural language, it can also process inquiries in natural language, although, with such big programs and dictionaries to store, on-line working seems at present a remote possibility.

In particular, is all well with the teletypewriter? Is it adequate for all necessary instructions? It is the sort of machine one would have for putting moderately long type-written messages into a store or a telegraph network. Therefore the inquirer could use it to establish his identity and to give one-word commands, but it is not quite so suitable for the quick thust-and-parry of a more advanced conversation with a computer. The user does not like to waste time moving between the display screen and the typewriter, or looking in two places at once. It would be ideal if he could speak his message into a microphone, but speech recognition, the technique of mechanically interpreting speech sounds and converting them into the same computer signals as the teletyped words, is still in its infancy. The most that can be done at present is for a machine to distinguish between a very few sounds, such as "yes" and "no," or "one," "two," "three," "four," and "five." Even then, it will make mistakes if different people speak to it, and it will make some wierd guess if any word not in its repertoire is spoken to it, whether in kindness or in anger.

Taking the combined skill of computers and users into account, the best way at present for some purposes is a display system with a light pen. This is a small photocell in a pencil-shaped holder, attached to a flexible cable leading by a separate channel into the computer. On the screen is displayed a small cross of light. When the photocell is brought close to it, a current is transmitted to the computer and carries information about the position of the light cross. A special program corrects this information as the light pen is moved, so that the light cross follows it. Thus the position of the cross constitutes an input signal to the computer, and the light-pen program contains suitable instructions that are dependent on this user-controlled signal. There are also ways of signaling in which the light pen locks into the light of some part or word of the main display. What the instructions are to be is the decision of the programmer. In the case of a textual display, the instructions can delete a word of text, make room for other words to be inserted by typewriter keyboard, or cause the computer to obey any one of a displayed list of commands. Instead of remembering or guessing what his choices are, the user is efficiently led through a tree of choices until he finds the service he wants. Heaven forbid that we should ever have to order our meals by computer, but just as an example, that sort of conversation would probably go in the following way (the computer displays the choices, the customer indicates his choice with the cross of the light pen):

Good day, sir,	Restaurant	Dinner
Which service?	Which meal?	First course?
valet	meal in room	soup of the day
hairdresser	breakfast	scampi +
banking	lunch	prawn cocktail

seat reservation	dinner +	spaghetti bolognaise
restaurant +		tomato juice
manager		no first course

and so on. The process would be swift, and there would be no chance of asking for anything the restaurant could not supply, provided that the chef had kept the computer up to date with what was available.

Evidently the designers of BOLD have this kind of conversation in mind when they state the scope, methodology, and approach of their research program. "The retrieval program will enable a user, seated at a remote inquiry station, to request documents in several ways. He may browse by specifying a broad classification category and requesting a display of the title and author of all documents in that category in much the same way as he would use a card catalog or wander through the open stacks (bookshelves). He may specify a combination of tag terms (descriptors) and request a display of titles and authors to meet these criteria. As the user defines a set, he is informed of the quantity of documents involved so that he may judge whether he wishes to increase or decrease this number by adding or deleting tag terms before requesting a display of the individual documents. The light pen is used on the display scope to designate a classification category, to reject data from the display during document search, to transfer data to the teletype, or to otherwise communicate directly with the computer."

Although present trends indicate an increasing application of light pens to on-line information retrieval, these may yet prove clumsier than some other alternative. In the last two paragraphs, the light pen has been shown to have only one rather simple application—to designate a choice of alternatives offered by the computer. With the sort of equipment on the market today, the user has to take up the pen, and bring it close to the display screen at the position that indicates his choice. There must be easier ways of showing a choice, occupying the user's hands and attention to a lesser extent. For example, close to the edge of the screen there could be a line of up to 20 push buttons or touch wires. The choice words shown on the screen could each have a line displayed, leading to the edge of the screen as near as possible to the appropriate button or touch wire. By touching a wire the user connects his body, a moderately good conductor of fairly high electrical capacity, to the circuitry and initiates a choice signal comparable to the signal he would make by pushing a button.

A Hospital Example

A special application of on-line information storage and retrieval will be in large hospitals where there are perhaps 1500 beds and 3000 daily visits from outpatients, with 100 people employed to look after 4 warehouses full of records, day and night. Typically, a given patient's record is needed in the ward or examination room at a few minutes' notice, but it is also wanted by dispensers, physiotherapists, X-ray departments, and administrators, some of whom are liable to keep their copies for several hours. It must be stored among the records of millions of other case histories, past and present. For both legal and medical reasons, as well as for the good of the patient, every record must be stored for many years, with the result that the Augean task of clearing out superfluous records cannot be attempted in manual systems. Many of the entries on a patient's record—those regarding observations, prescriptions, and other forms of treatment—must be made on the spot by the doctor in charge; no safe way of batching or delaying the entry of these decisions has been found.

Beginning in two wards only, Professor J. Anderson of King's College Hospital, London, is aiming to abolish 99 per cent of paper work in the hospital, and to use a single multi-access computer and disk files for the records. The changeover must be clean and effective, without requiring doctors and nurses to record everything twice during any transition period, and Professor Anderson took six years over the preparatory work alone. He found that a radical standardization of terminology was essential, so he devised one and taught it to every new generation of medical students. He also devised a very compact record format in which a case history can be written

```
                    ONE CHOICE
  1   HISTORY
  2   PAST HISTORY
  3   FAMILY HISTORY
  4   SOCIAL HISTORY
  5   BODILY FUNCTIONS
  6   HABITS
 ●7   PHYSICAL EXAMINATION
  8   DIAGNOSIS
  9   TREATMENT
 10   MANAGEMENT
```

```
                    ONE CHOICE

  PHYSICAL EXAMINATION
   1   TRUNDLE
  ●2   WADDINGTON
```

The sets of words shown on these pages represent separate displays appearing consecutively on a cathode-ray screen as part of an on-line information storage and retrieval system being developed by Professor J. Anderson at King's College Hospital, London. The system is designed to replace the majority of paper work concerning patient data (examination results, case histories, etc.) by a number of conversational terminals linked to a multiaccess computer and disk file. The terminals (as shown on page 48) are silent in use and compact enough to accompany consultants on their ward rounds. When a doctor wishes to enter information about one of his patients, he types in an author code, equivalent to a personal keyword, which will be entered into the store with the final compiled information. The example shown here begins at the top lefthand corner of this page. The first display offers a wide range of categories.

```
  P PEDLESEN          25 M 66219G
  PHYSICAL EXAMINATION
  —RESPIRATORY :TRACHEA CENTRAL :MOVEMENT
  S EQUAL :PERCUSSION NOTE NORMAL :BREATH
  SOUNDS NORMAL —INSPECTION —RESPIRATORY R
  ATE :] 60 [PER MINUTE
```

```
                         NUMERALS
  P PEDLESEN          25 M 66219G
  PHYSICAL EXAMINATIONRESPIRATORY RATE
            ]   [ PERMINUTE
```

ONE CHOICE

PHYSICAL EXAMINATION
1   G J HOWE
2   W TYSON
3   F S COULMAN
4   E R WREN
● 5   P PEDLESEN

ONE CHOICE

P PEDLESEN   25 M 66219G
PHYSICAL EXAMINATION
1   GENERAL   11 PAEDIATRICS
2   CARDIOVASCULAR   12 OBSTETRICS
● 3   RESPIRATORY   13 GYNAECOLOGY
4   GASTROINTESTINAL   14 ENDOCRINOLOGY
5   NEUROLOGICAL   15 DERMATOLOGY
6   MUSCULOSKELETAL   16 VENEREOLOGY
7   UROLOGICAL
8   GENERAL SURGERY
9   OPHTHALMOLOGY
10 EAR NOSE AND THROAT

→

The circle indicates that he has chosen to enter details of a physical examination by depressing key 7 on the keyboard. Immediately a selection is made, the next display appears. This one happens to be a choice between two wards. The remainder of the routine is easy to follow, being carried out to record details of the patient's respiratory condition. The final display is entered into the store and can be retrieved at any terminal.

←

CHOICES

P PEDLESEN   25 M 66219G
PHYSICAL EXAMINATIONRESPIRATORY
● 1   TRACHEA CENTRAL
● 2   MOVEMENTS EQUAL
● 3   PERCUSSION NOTE NORMAL
● 4   BREATH SOUNDS NORMAL
5   NO ADVENTITIOUS SOUNDS
6   SPECIALITY DISPLAY SYSTEM

ONE CHOICE

P PEDLESEN   25 M 66219G
PHYSICAL EXAMINATIONINSPECTION
● 1   RESPIRATORY RATE
2   RESPIRATORY RHYTHM
3   RESPIRATORY CHARACTER
4   CHEST SHAPE
5   CHEST MOVEMENTS
6   CHEST WALL SPECIAL FEATURES
7   SPUTUM

ONE CHOICE

P PEDLESEN   25 M 66219G
PHYSICAL EXAMINATIONRESPIRATORY
● 1   INSPECTION
2   PALPATION
3   PERCUSSION
4   AUSCULTATION

in half the usual number of words, and include more than the usual amount of information—for example, comments from the general practitioner about the patient's normal environment, or emotional and social background.

The conversational terminals will be visual display units, similar to that shown (with view of author's head) on page 48. A terminal will accompany each consultant on his ward rounds, and there will be fixed terminals at all the places where information about patients is needed or generated. Printed output will be obtained in the dispensaries and administrative departments with teletypewriters in addition to the display units. The cost of a full scheme on these lines will be no more than at present, but Professor Anderson foresees a significant decrease in rates of errors, omissions, and duplications, and a valuable reorganization and reform of hospital administration. Other benefits are that it will be possible by batch processing to erase records or dump them on magnetic tape when they are no longer needed. No well-founded statistical studies of records are possible with manual filing in order of patient's name, but the computer's ability to search a file by many different categories will revolutionize the study of case histories.

Long-range Data Communication

Although the characters on the screen or the teletyped roll are alphanumeric, the signals that come from the computer to produce them are always in binary form—in computer terms, *data*. In an ideal system, a great central store of information, controlled by nearby computers, would be accessible from anywhere in the country. Such a system would permit the most efficient store organization and use of computer, the most elaborate conversational programs, and the best service to users. What are the difficulties in sending data over long distances? Nothing to worry about, although the facilities could be cheaper and less troublesome than those we have at present. The on-line system of computer access was hardly under way when long-distance tests were made. To get on-line to a computer the only method we have at present is to pick up a modified telephone and dial the computer's phone number.

A signal comes back, meaning "You're connected," the user presses an extra button on his telephone set, and the teletype machine starts into action. As soon as there was one experimental system in Massachusetts and another in Texas, the two groups of computer scientists began using the ordinary telephone service to get on-line to the other computer, and it worked very successfully. (They then worked on various safety devices to prevent valuable programs from being damaged by outside interference.)

Although usable, the common telephone network is hardly the ideal channel for communicating with a distant computer. Dialing a number is known as "forward switching," because the signals transmitted to the exchange as the dial unwinds back to its rest position are used to select first the exchange and then the number of the person you are calling. From then until one of you hangs up, the line joining you is all yours. This system is quite convenient for speech but, as we shall see, unnecessarily wasteful for data transmission. There is also the expense, for the data senders, of installing a modem at each end of the communication line. The *modem* is a box of electronic equipment that accepts a digital signal and uses it to vary the amplitude, frequency, or phase of an alternating current carrier wave; in technical terms it modulates the wave. At the receiving end, a similar box demodulates the signal, that is, converts it to the original digital signal. Modems are necessary to protect the ordinary telephone user against "noise" that might be induced by digital signals in adjacent circuits. Telegraph and telex networks, which do not need modems, cannot handle the high speed of data transmission required for a computer-based system.

The Post Office in the United Kingdom is investigating the possibilities of a revolutionary system of data communication that uses the property of computers known as multiaccess to accept signals from many sources at the same time and to deal with them sequentially at very high speed without any confusion. The practical advantages of such a system are that it makes extremely economical use of the cables (whose laying and repairing cost is one of the heavy expenses of all public telephone corporations) and that it can continue to function while some of the cables are out of action through damage or maintenance operations. An experimental data-communication network is being established at the National Physical Laboratory that will include five or six computers of various sizes, a very large disk file, and specimens of all the more important additional equipment that would be needed for a national data-communication network. While helping in the normal computing and data-processing work of the laboratory it will provide basic experience that will help in the design of a national network.

The two very special features of this type of data-transmission system are that it uses small computers, called *nodal computers*, in place of the telephone exchanges, and that the messages are sent more like mailed letters than telephone calls. After all, ordinary mail is just another form of communication. It is input by the writer into a street mailbox, and output by the mailman through a door, after it has been transmitted by the postal transmission system. The postal system can be described as a "sort, store, and forward" system. Any particular letter goes first into a sorting office, where it is stored in a container together with other letters with approximately the same destination. This batch travels to a second sorting office nearer the destination, where a re-sort takes place and the original letter finds itself in another container along with letters having very nearly the same destination. It reaches a third sorting office, where mail is re-sorted into districts, and a mailman picks up the mail of one district and delivers each letter to its exact destination.

The proposed system for transmission of data is a "store and forward" system. There is no need for sorting at any stage because the message is given individual treatment—indeed if it is a long message it is dissected into fragments of suitable length and each fragment is sent separately to the destination. The fragments are quite small, corresponding to no more than a line of typing or a line on a display screen, the reason being that many messages will be smaller than this anyway, and at every stage in the transmission a check for errors must be made and, if an error is detected, the whole fragment must be re-transmitted over that stage.

How does the user mail his message? At a terminal tele-typewriter or a display typewriter connected to the system he types his own identification, the identification of the addressee (it may be a central computer used by his firm, for instance), and the message. Within a few seconds the signal appears on his equipment "message delivered," if he has asked for it. The operations corresponding to putting the message into an envelope and dropping it into a street mailbox are not in fact done by the user. They are done by a local (and more expensive) computer that serves perhaps 200 terminals, called an *interface computer*. (*Interface* is a recently coined word for the often complex arrangements made for joining two sub-systems together.) The interface computer presents the message back to the sender if required for checking, divides it into *packets*—a name for the fragments of suitable length for transmission—and attaches to each packet various markers in the system's own code. Without disturbing the content of the packet in any way, it adds a "begin packet" signal, the address of origin and destination, and a sum check number for error detection. This operation corresponds to putting each packet into an envelope and addressing it. The sum check is simply a record of the sum of all the word-numbers in the packet, and if the sum is different at the other end an error signal will be sent back, causing the message to be repeated.

The interface computer posts the first packet by sending it to the nearest nodal computer; when the sum check tallies, the interface computer wipes out its stored version of the first packet and starts to post the second. The nodal computer starts the packet on its journey by sending it to any node conveniently on its route. The second node finds a third, and so on, until the packet reaches the interface computer serving its destina-tion terminal. From here the packets, shorn of their markers and in their correct order, are transmitted to the terminal.

The meaning of the phrase "any node conveniently on its route" can be envisaged from the diagram on page 161, an imaginary map of the nodes and link lines needed to operate

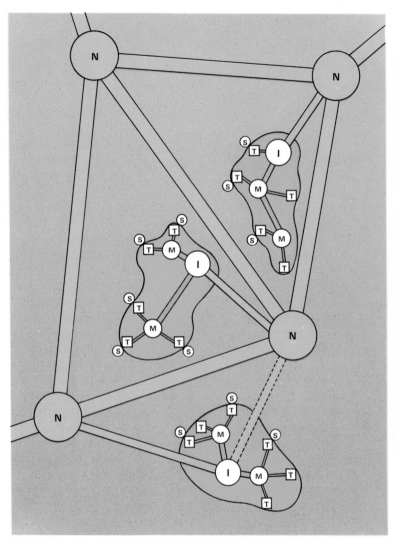

The diagram above shows the interrelation of the main parts of the public data network described in the text. The node computers (N) and the long-distance network are shown in blue, and local network areas around an interface computer (I) are shown in red. Subscribers (S) in the outside world (represented by green tone) communicate by way of visual display terminals (T) through multiplexers (M) to an interface computer. Multiplexers allow several messages to be transmitted simultaneously per channel and are used to economize in total cable needed between a number of terminals and an interface computer. The map opposite shows possible positions of nodes and link lines for such a network in the United Kingdom.

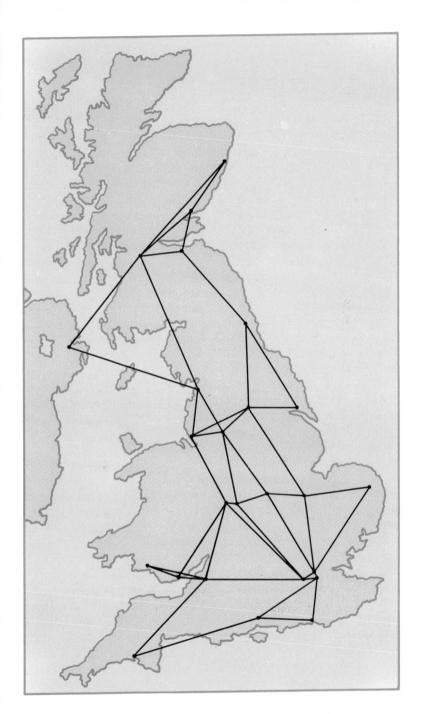

this "store and forward" system in the United Kingdom. Between any two nodes there is always a choice of routes, and the nodal computers are capable of finding a good route, making allowance for heavy traffic at certain nodes, certain links out of action, or even certain nodes out of action.

Each computer in the system, whether nodal or interface, will have storage available for between 20 and 100 packets, because there will be times when messages are coming into a computer faster than they are being sent out. There are also times when the same packet of information is stored simultaneously in both the sending and the receiving computer—while error checks are being made, and errors corrected.

Present estimates indicate that a packet could be transmitted between remote places in the United Kingdom and a central computer in less than one-tenth of a second; and the cost of the service to the Post Office might be between one- and two-tenths of a penny (or a cent) per packet. Reliability should be considerably higher than that obtainable by current systems, and overall maintenance of the system much easier—even though there are computers to be maintained. Naturally both increased reliability and decreased maintenance costs contribute to the low overall cost of the service.

The most important users of a public data-transmission network are likely to be the banks, which have the need to update customers' accounts daily, and to refer inquiries on-line to the central computer whenever they arise. British banking is organized into six large banks and four smaller ones, although the present tendency is for mergers and the formation of even fewer and larger banks. Typically, a large bank has 2000 branches scattered fairly evenly over the whole country. Already it is necessary for each branch to have a direct data line to the central computer, and so much underground telephone cable has to be rented that a form of line-sharing among neighboring branches is used, called *poling*; at the junction of each set of line-sharers there is an automatic poling switch that offers the shared line to each branch in turn, moving on when it receives an "end of transmission" signal. The banks already recognize that the present system is unnecessarily clumsy and failure-prone, and that in five years or less they will have to change it for something more permanent. One advantage of the proposed system is that it will work with various types of terminal equipment, including all that are at present favored by the banks.

Other large users of a data network on-line are likely to be mail-order firms, chain stores, ticket and travel agencies including the airlines, hotels, weather forecasters, and betting shops. Their type of message and method of using the data network would be quite varied, but the network would have no difficulty (as far as can be foreseen) in handling all such traffic. The Post Office would be able, when the time came, to use the network for all inland telegrams and telex messages; in the more distant future even telephone calls could be added to the list, in spite of their analogue nature.

Clearly a data-transmission network in this or some other form is likely to arise because of the demands of important commercial transactions. A usage equivalent to about one-hundredth of the total telephone traffic can already be fore-seen; this will entail the transmission of some 50 million packets per day, but once the system is installed its usage will certainly grow, as will the applications of central multiaccess computers and data stores. At this point the obvious question is: will our library information services benefit from the existence of such a public data-communication system?

Libraries and the Data Network

With books, documents, and libraries in their present form, information services will not be big users of a data network, because the total amount of traffic they provide will be small in comparison with that of the big commercial users. On the other hand the ability to consult stores of bibliographic information on-line from a distance is likely to give a boost to librarianship such as it has never had before. Properly applied, it will lead to an enormous improvement in the service that can be offered to inquirers of all kinds; and the result of such an improvement is likely to be a manifold increase in the number of inquiries.

Every well-developed country now has many individual libraries. Each library holds a collection of books and documents, together with records of bibliographic information about the collection. From the indexes, the bibliographies, and the shelves, an inquirer's needs can be met, more or less effectively and more or less quickly, within the limitations of the particular collection and its associated classified information. In addition, libraries usually have information about the collections of other libraries, sometimes with classified bibliographies but rarely with indexes; so they can tell an inquirer something about documents that may interest him. This is about all the retrospective service that can usually be offered. The current-awareness service, as we have seen in Chapter 5, is different; but, because it functions within the same classification framework, the service is comparable in value and accuracy.

But imagine what a difference on-line data communication with a central store and computer from a wide area at low cost would make to these services. The following conclusions seem to be obvious. (1) The area in communication with the center would grow, to cover first the state, then the whole country, then the whole world. (2) Abstracting, indexing, and bibliographies would be done by specialists in their homes or offices and the results sent from their local library terminal to the central store and library. (3) Retrospective inquiries would be made at local library terminals, narrowed down by conversation, and clinched by examination of abstracts on the teletypewriter or display. When it became clear what documents the inquirer needed, he would receive instructions on how to order facsimiles. If speed was essential and cost no object he could receive a transcript of the entire document over the network, assuming it was stored in its entirety. (4) Instead of there being one classification system to help in the searches, there would be many. There are many today, but each refers to a particular collection of documents and suits some, but by no means all, the users of that collection. The task of establishing more than one system for any one collection has proved daunting: it is hard enough to build up the indexes for one system and keep them up to date with new documents, but it is very much harder to devise new systems and introduce them. We have seen that ideally each inquirer should have his own classification system. Even with a highly mechanized central service this would not be possible, but it would be possible to have many systems, each suited to a particular class of inquirer. (5) Sophistication—the elaboration in range and detail of the services from the center—would grow in proportion to the demand. Why bother to have a whole document copied and posted to an inquirer who only wants to read a paragraph or examine one diagram? Show him the relevant parts on a display, page by page if necessary, until he has what he wants in front of him. Why stick to ordinary documents? Perhaps separate centers could store engineering or architectural drawings, and be connected to a central computer equipped with computer-aided design programs. Or perhaps, for patent information, legal case reports, and local and central government proceedings, both special centers and the general centers would need to keep the information: the special centers would have computers with specialized programs, and the general center ordinary library facilities.

The above list is unlikely to be complete. Most of the services that are now idle pipe dreams, because of their cost and the small clientele, become realizable when they can reach users in the entire world at no extra outlay. The ideas that are now in abeyance or being timidly studied in a theoretical way will receive full-blooded support, and when long-range information retrieval gets into its stride the present era will be looked back on as a period of doldrums.

Another likely result is a decline in the printing industry. We saw in Chapter 5 that a whole year may be lost between the writing of a primary scientific article and its appearance in a journal. Some of this delay is tolerable, but if the journal were held in a central computer store, there would be a saving of time at every stage. Each article could be put into the store when it was ready, and its abstract could be published in traditional form along with abstracts from other comparable journals in the next issue of a weekly abstracts journal. Its descriptors could go at once into the indexing systems, and everyone whose profile they matched could be notified at once. People who asked to see the whole article could be sent a transcription by the central services and, perhaps a little later, a facsimile copy of the article complete with illustrations—made from a carefully typed or printed version. This would fit in well with the way many scientists now send for facsimiles or offprints of all articles that interest them and store them in accordance with their own classification system.

If there is a decline in the printing of primary scientific articles by traditional methods, possibly libraries will decline too as stores for documents. On the other hand they may simply change their role a little. We are here concerned with libraries that collect a large number of journals, index the articles, and produce them when required for their clients. In a data transmission era the same libraries are likely to make retrieval easier by collecting facsimiles, perhaps several copies of each article, classifying them, and so avoiding the awkwardness of having diverse articles in each volume.

More likely, however, is that the traditional scientific libraries will change their role quite drastically, and become true information centers of the kind indicated in Chapter 3. In a world where there is on-line communication between libraries and a central comprehensive store of bibliographic information, a remarkable development of information centers is foreseeable. Every specialist library belonging to a corporation or government department is likely first to install communication terminals, and then to expand with demand. Its reference librarians will be avidly consulted and will use the terminals to improve and consolidate their specialist knowledge. The library will become a mission-oriented information center, and perhaps help in preparing information from new documents for the central store. Similarly every discipline-oriented library belonging to an educational or national research establishment is likely to become a discipline-oriented information center.

In conclusion, let us review the chain of development considered in this chapter and note any weak links it may have. It begins with computers designed (chiefly in their software) to allow multiaccess from a number of users at the same time. Along with this goes a choice of high-level languages for conversation, and a choice of terminal equipment. So far there are no weak links, because everything is here already, and being used both industrially and in experimental and teaching establishments. The next requirement is a large and growing central store of bibliographic information. At present it is not central, not large, and not growing in a suitable way. Before it can be given a suitable nucleus and encouraged to grow, a great deal of human organization is needed, nationally and internationally, to coordinate the efforts already being made, to augment them, and to unify the end product—a central store of information. This is certainly one weak link in the chain, because its development must be prompted by government action: such coordinated efforts do not come naturally by ordinary economic or democratic processes. Government action will undoubtedly be easier if there is a clear goal to be aimed at and a clear method of getting there. As it happens, both the goal and the method will become dazzlingly clear if one more link is forged: a long-range data-communication network for public use. This need not be identical with what has just been described; the problem is not one of design, but of economic development. Libraries and information scientists cannot make an economic case for a public network on the grounds that scientific and technical awareness will thereby be better to the tune of so many million pounds or dollars. They have no means of doing the calculations, and any engineer could see immediately that their contribution to the traffic of a data network would be very small compared with the capacity available. So the economic pressure for the establishment of a suitable network must come from elsewhere, and information retrieval must be content to wait like a jackal for its share of the spoils. The likely origins of economic pressure— banks, chain stores, and so on—have already been indicated, but it has not been possible to assess how much pressure they will generate. If for some reason this vital link in the chain fails to be forged, a much slower and less predictable line of development seems to be the destiny of information retrieval.

7 Fact Retrieval

The progress of computer science may be compared with the development of an ideally intelligent man. In his childhood he is, of course, an infant prodigy. His brain is well ordered and his computations are neat and easily checked for errors. But his data base is ridiculously small; for several years he has been busy learning the arts of muscular control, communication, and social behavior, living at home, and not noticing how the world works. So he occupies himself with pursuits that require little data, and becomes a pure mathematician and a musician. As he grows older his experience widens. More and more facts go into his data base and, in thinking about what he observes, he stores them in some sort of semantic order, which is much better than the time-serial order in which the observations come in. Eventually he finds that his mathematical pursuits no longer satisfy him, and he turns to problems that are more general, less tangible, less provable. If he remembers to acquire the art of explaining

This is Somerset House in London. Part of it contains all records concerning births, marriages, divorces, and deaths for all people born in England and Wales since 1837. Aspiring aristocrats can establish the identity of their ancestors, and the answers they receive are facts retrieved from a massive amount of data. This chapter explores the possibilities of computer-based fact retrieval systems that could not only speed up tasks such as this but also aid scientific research by revealing facts not attainable by human efforts alone.

himself to those whose intelligence is not so ideal, he will be the benefactor he is expected to be. The computer is not a genius and could not outwit even a moron, but its life story is similar. It began as a mathematician, and very soon earned its living by doing sums. Today it can not only manage large stores of data, but is beginning to handle them in more general ways. It is acquiring the art of communicating with people who cannot wait while batches of data are being processed, and it should soon be an even greater asset than it is already.

As we saw in Chapters 4 and 5, the computer can help libraries in two ways. With a highly complex program, and only 10,000 or so documents as working data, it can produce by batch-processing methods a thesaurus or descriptor system suitable for the classification of documents. Using simple programs, and a file of very many "documents" (the bibliographic data and descriptors for a whole library), it can match these descriptors with those of an inquiry, and output the bibliographic data of matching documents. Batch-processing methods are used in retrospective searching, partly because in this way an efficient use is made of the computer's time. The same programs, working on the newest additions to the document file, serve equally well for matching these documents with individual profiles and producing an SDI service. Here batch processing is also used, because the new documents and profiles are suitable for a single run, monopolizing the entire computer. However, in Chapter 6 we saw the efficiency of retrospective searches made by on-line use of a multiaccess computer, not hogging a great deal of the computer's time, but narrowing down the inquiry, giving the inquirer some immediate information, and ensuring that the bulk of the final print-out from the document file would be useful. Conversation of this type requires elaborate programs, but most of these are part of the software of multiaccess computers, and not specifically related to the library inquiries whose programs remain nearly as simple as for batch processing. In the present chapter we shall again consider tasks that require conversation with a computer, but these demand a more elaborate use of the file of information, and use more difficult programs. The tasks, seen as applications of the computer, range from the merely novel to the extremely subtle, but they share the common name of "fact retrieval."

The distinction between information retrieval and the simplest kind of fact retrieval can be seen in the following examples. (1) Request to a librarian: make a complete list of all books, papers, and technical reports in the library that deal with the subject "Resonance radiation and excited atoms." (2) Request to public records in Somerset House, London: "List with their interrelations the common ancestors born after 1800 of Bertrand Russell and J. M. Keynes."

The answers to both requests are information, but in the first case the inquirer does not know, as a result, any more about the subject of his inquiry (he merely has a list of documents), whereas in the second he expects to know all about it.

Although fact retrieval is new in name, it is a common activity of the human brain when dealing with relatively small stores of data. We find that historic achievements in many departments of science have used methods of fact retrieval, but first we need to be able to distinguish between those scientific methods that are fact retrieval and those that are not.

In the compendium *Frontiers of Science and Philosophy* (edited by Robert G. Colodny), Ernst Caspari, writing on the "Conceptual Basis of the Biological Sciences," makes the following broad assertions: "The raw material of all sciences consists in statements about observations. The task of any science is to bring these statements about observations into a systematic order which can be grasped by the human mind. The unspoken assumption behind this ordering activity is the belief that some kind of order which can be formulated by the human mind exists in reality. . . .

"In biology two methods for the obtaining of observations and ordering the statements about them are used. One consists in the comparison of existing organisms, species, or organs with each other, or with the remains of extinct organisms. The other one derives its statements about observation from experiments. Both types of statement form an integral part of biology. The method of comparison leads to the establishment of similarities and dissimilarities between objects, individuals or structures. It has sometimes been called the 'order-analytical' method. The experimental method leads ideally to the establishment of causal connections, and is therefore called the 'causal-analytical' method."

The first of these two methods is very similar to, if not identical with, fact retrieval. Caspari points out that the same dichotomy applies to the inorganic sciences, and it is important to consider carefully what he is driving at. A physicist would probably be more interested in the *methods* of making "statements about observations"—for instance, in whether they are mathematical, graphic, or verbal. But Caspari disregards the form or code used for the statements; and this attitude meets with the approval of computer scientists, who are accustomed to seeing the same information expressed in a variety of ways in the course of being processed. Instead, he makes a distinction between the ways in which the observations are processed, which partly depend on the methods by which they are gathered in the first place. If they are gathered by observation, such as recording the habits of wild animals or the spectra of the stars, there is often too little control over the order in which the observations come in. If they are the results of experiments, the order can often be controlled, and relatively few observations may be needed to prove a point.

One famous experiment is performed by schoolboys and schoolgirls, who vary the voltage across the ends of a resistor (as shown opposite), measure the variations in the current, and rediscover Ohm's Law (that the current through a resistor is in direct proportion to the voltage difference between its ends). By consciously varying the voltage, the experimenter has controlled the current, but if he thinks that voltage always controls or causes current he will become entangled in a fallacy. There are many cases when the current through a resistor causes the voltage between its ends; an *ammeter* with a shunt is one such case (as shown opposite). Thus it is advisable to assume no deep philosophical implications when this is called the *casual-analytical* method.

In some investigations it is not possible to make experi-

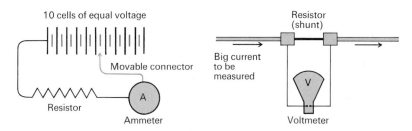

10 cells of equal voltage

Movable connector

Resistor

Ammeter

Resistor
(shunt)

Big current
to be
measured

Voltmeter

The diagram at above left shows how Ohm's Law is proved in the classroom. Varying the voltage across the ends of a resistor produces variations in the current registered by the ammeter (A). This may suggest that voltage always controls current. The diagram at above right illustrates a relationship not revealed in the first diagram, i.e. that a current can control the voltage between the ends of a resistor (when it is used as a shunt). In this case the voltmeter and shunt are used as an ammeter. These examples underline the careful interpretation necessary for facts revealed by causal-analytical methods.

ments like this. Consider a case in which Ohm's Law might be rediscovered without any experiments, using only observations. The observer might measure the currents and voltages associated with all the resistors in his television set while it is in operation. He would not at this stage prove Ohm's Law, but if he also measured the heat generated per minute within each resistor, he would achieve a combination of Ohm's and Joule's laws. Then, if he examined a set of resistors all of which carried equal currents, and listed them in order of their heat generation, he would find the order the same as the order of their voltages. Going on to other sets of resistors carrying other currents, he would hit upon a property that seemed to be characteristic of each resistor. Whether or not he called this property the *resistance*, he would now be in a position to state both Ohm's and Joule's laws. He has discovered the laws by a method of *order analysis* (one of many), and the way he thought about and processed the observations was *order-analytical*. It is typical that his way to the simple truth has been rather arduous.

Order-analytical methods may be clumsier, but they are more versatile than causal-analytical methods. They can handle data that result from experiment or from passive observation. Most of meteorology and the whole of archaeology and astronomy have been developed by order analysis. They are also highly suited to data that are wholly or in part non-numerical, as in agriculture, linguistics, and psychology. Their clumsiness has been partly relieved in the last 40 years by improvements in technique, notably in statistics and structure analysis. In this chapter we are considering, among other things, whether they can be helped by the conversational use of computers.

We shall begin by examining a varied selection of scientific investigations, already completed, that are order-analytical. Later we shall consider two systems, still in the research and development stage, that are regarded by computer scientists as "fact retrieval." The object is to prove (by an order-analytical method, incidentally) that all order-analytical investigations are forms of fact retrieval. If this generalization is broadly true, the variety of order-analytical investigations that have been achieved so far will indicate that systems of computer-aided fact retrieval have a tremendous potential of usefulness in scientific research of the future. En route we shall see that their usefulness is by no means restricted to what we usually think of as scientific research.

(1) *Mendeleeff's Periodic Table.* The systematization of chemical phenomena began in 1803 at Manchester when Dalton devised an atomic hypothesis that would justify the Lavoisier law of conservation of mass, and two laws about the proportions in which the elements combine. In 1811 Avogadro found a way of recasting a new law by Gay-Lussac that supported and clarified Dalton's atomic theory and led to a method of determining atomic weights—the relative masses of the elementary atoms. After 50 years of debate and confusion these ideas gained credence, and atomic weights were determined in earnest. Before long there was a sizable list of elements, for each of which were known the atomic weight and a collection of physical and chemical properties. That is to say, there was a corpus of information of the form: name of element, atomic weight, melting point, and other physical properties, and a list of elements combining with it in

the ratios 1:1, 2:1, etc. This was ideal for treatment by order analysis, and several people tried, with only partial success. After the event we can say that an obvious way to try is to arrange the elements in order of their atomic weights and look for any sort of regularity in their other properties. At the time it was far from obvious, but the Russian chemist Mendeleeff in St. Petersburg (now Leningrad) made it his business "to look about and write down the elements with their atomic weights" and was soon convinced that the properties of the elements are in periodic dependence upon their atomic weights.

When Mendeleeff announced his law in 1869, there were gaps in his periodic table corresponding to elements that had not yet been found. There were also gross errors in some of the stated atomic weights, due to mistaken judgments about valencies (the numerical proportions of the atoms of two different elements in a compound). To make his periodic table consistent, Mendeleeff proposed gross changes in the atomic

Mendeleeff's periodic table, shown below, is a good example of the value of order-analytical research. The Russian chemist left spaces in his table that he considered would be occupied by elements yet to be discovered. He predicted their properties on the grounds of the nature of elements similarly placed in terms of groups and series. The discovery of scandium, gallium, and germanium— which occupy the positions marked with 44, 68, and 72 respectively—was a triumphant confirmation of his law.

es	Group I	Group II	Group III	Group IV	Group V	Group VI	Group VII	Group VIII
	H 1							
	Li 7	Be 9·4	B 11	C 12	N 14	O 16	F 19	
	Na 23	Mg 24	Al 27·3	Si 28	P 31	S 32	Cl 35·5	
	K 39	Ca 40	—44	Ti 48	V 51	Cr 52	Mn 55	Fe 56, Co 59,
	Cu 63	Zn 65	—68	—72	As 75	Se 78	Br 80	Ni 59, Cu 63
	Rb 85	Sr 87	Yt 88	Zr 90	Nb 94	Mo 96	—100	Ru 104, Rh 104,
	Ag 108	Cd 112	In 113	Sn 118	Sb 122	Te 125	I 127	Pd 106, Ag 108
	Cs 133	Ba 137	Di 138	Ce 140	—	—	—	— — — —
	—	—	Er 178	La 180	Ta 182	W 184	—	Os 195, Ir 197,
	Au 199	Hg 200	Tl 204	Pb 270	Bi 208	—	—	Pt 198, Au 199
	—	—	—	Th 231	—	U 240	—	— — — —

weights of three elements—indium, beryllium, and uranium—and predicted the discovery of three new elements. His description of their properties went into considerable detail, including density, color, metallicity, and properties of their oxides, chlorides, and organic compounds.

The triumphant justification of Mendeleeff's law came through the discovery of all three missing elements in minerals within the next 15 years, their properties being substantially the same as he had predicted. These elements are called scandium, gallium, and germanium (see the table shown on page 175).

From then on, it is true, there was little order analysis in the development of atomic theory. It proceeded by experimental observation of radioactivity, artificial collisions between nucleons, the photoelectric effect, etc., to our modern science of fundamental particles, but the initial breakthrough had been made by order analysis.

(2) *Air Pollution in Towns.* The investigation I completed in the late 1940s, into nature's methods of removing atmospheric pollution from the air of towns, can also be cited as an example of order analysis. In a smoky city, every exposed surface becomes dirty in a short time: buildings, streets, vegetation, interiors of houses, materials, clothing, and so on. It might be imagined that enough dirt is collected in this way to account for all that is emitted from the chimneys and industrial processes, but this is far from true. I started by making a large number of systematic measurements of pollution, for three years, in many parts of a town of 250,000 inhabitants and in its rural surroundings, and found that the concentration of smoke within the town varied greatly from day to day, over a range of about 20 to 1. Several different order-analytical methods were used to find the explanation of such a large variation, including the statistical treatment that had been developed by R. A. Fisher in his work on agricultural research. This showed that the changes in smoke concentration were mainly brought about by changes in weather conditions: temperature, rain, wind velocity, and air turbulence. Of these the last-named was easily the most important. On days when

a measurable wind of any speed was blowing, the highest turbulence corresponded with the lowest pollution, and the lowest turbulence corresponded with a ten-fold increase in smoke concentration. Fog and very high pollution occurred when there was little wind and very little turbulence in the air within 500 ft. of the ground. What was making the air reasonably pure in clear weather was not the deposition of smoke, but its removal by air currents; not so much its removal horizontally by the wind as its dispersion upward by atmospheric turbulence. As the smoke-laden air was dispersed upward and away, fresh air from heights far above the chimney tops was taking its place.

Although the methods of data processing were statistical, involving correlation coefficients, partial regressions, significance tests, and suchlike devices, they were not fundamentally different from straightforward classification. For example, in some tests the pollution measurements on days with particular ranges of wind velocity were studied separately; summer was always separated from winter, and weekends from weekdays. Perhaps the chief difference of this kind of research from that of Mendeleeff, or from taxonomy, is that there is no limit to the number of observations that may be used.

(3) *Classifying the Stars*. For many centuries, the only observations men could make on the stars were their positions and their brightness, i.e. their apparent magnitude. By 1900 many of their distances had been measured by parallax, allowing the calculation of their absolute magnitudes in terms of the luminosity of the sun as a unit. At the same time their spectra had been observed. Rather interestingly, the astronomers found it convenient to classify the stars according to their type of spectrum, assigning seven letters to the seven broad subdivisions of spectral type. (The diagram on page 178 shows only six; the category O was added later.)

In 1913 the American astronomer H. N. Russell and the Danish astronomer E. Hertzsprung pointed out that if absolute magnitudes (the measure of the brightness of a star at a given distance) as ordinates are plotted against spectral types as abscissae, the general configuration of the plotted points is

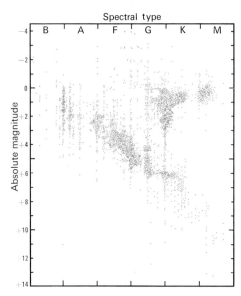

The Hertzsprung-Russell diagram (shown at left), although a very simple manipulation of already-known data about stars, is remarkably effective in that it immediately classifies them into two distinct groups and a number of types. The so-called "giant" stars at the top right of the diagram are very bright irrespective of their spectral type, while the "main sequence" is composed of stars whose brightness decreases as their spectral type moves toward the redder, cooler end. This representation prompted scientists to theorize about the evolution of stars, and initiated a great deal of research in the newly formulated science of astrophysics.

along two lines (see the diagram on this page). Thus their order analysis immediately divided the majority of stars into two sets: the members of one set are all very bright, irrespective of their type of spectrum, while the members of the other set seem to have a linearly decreasing brightness as their spectral type shifts toward the redder, cooler end.

This simple-looking piece of classification initiated an immense development in the scope of astronomy. People were able to theorize about the evolution of stars, and to test their theories as well. The odd stars that did not belong to either set were studied, revolutionary ideas about states of matter developed, and astrophysics emerged as the Cinderella of science, with a sequence of great mathematicians in the role of Prince Charming.

The Hertzsprung-Russell diagram was discovered by a simple order analysis of certain properties of stars. More elaborate statistical techniques might have been used equally successfully, but they were unnecessary. They would probably be necessary if there were other distinguishable sets of stars embedded, for instance, in the downward-sloping set of the diagram. Let us suppose that an empirical search for sets was worth making—how best could it be done? Probably by storing a large sample of the stellar data in a core store of a computer and making trials with it, conversationally—but here we are anticipating one of the conclusions of this chapter.

Computerized Fact Retrieval

As has been indicated already, fact-retrieval tasks range from the relatively simple to the almost impossible. Asa Kasher draws the distinction in "Data Retrieval by Computer: a Critical Survey," an article in the book of readings *The Growth of Knowledge*, edited by Manfred Kochen. He warns system designers not to expect easy, quick, or profitable results from work on fact retrieval, particularly if the input messages are to be in natural language. Schools of linguistics have so far only succeeded in showing up, without curing them, the various kinds of ambiguity in ordinary language, which we—with our appreciation of context and meaning—can easily resolve, but for which there is no computer algorithm. Scientists are guilty of a tendency to ignore the findings and difficulties of linguistics; they are culpably vague about language itself, about the relation between a question and its answer, and about the determination of relevance. He reminds them of Alan Turing's paper "Computing Machinery and Intelligence" (1950), describing how a computer must fail any precisely prepared test related to the proposition "machines can think."

For such reasons, Kasher does not believe that there is any real hope for success, in the near future, of systems of fact retrieval "purporting to deal equally well with any field of discourse, or for that matter with one extensive field." Research is needed on the syntax and semantics of natural languages, methods of formalization and structuring of the fields of discourse, and nonclassical logic, with the aim of producing computable processes. On the other hand, he claims that there is hope for success in fact-retrieval systems for special purposes, which employ a carefully organized data base, a reliable technical language, and a competent inference mechanism. To appreciate what he means, it is best to consider two systems, one of which is down to earth, and the other more ambitious. *Fact Retrieval from a Police Data Base.* The research program of the Division of Computer Science at the National Physical Laboratory includes a project by Dr. D. M. Yates, described in the NPL Annual Report for 1968, whose initial aims are: (1) To develop a computer-based question-answering system that allows effective and varied use of data compiled and selected by police staff. (The requests are in a technical language: replies are in a humanly readable form.) (2) As far as possible, to make the system versatile so that it can be used on other data bases with different queries.

A data base consists of files (stores separately accessible from a computer). In the police application there are five files: one for cars, one for men, and so on. Each file contains many entries (the man file, for example, might contain 30,000 entries, one for each man). The data within an entry is an organized collection of attribute-value pairs (e.g. color of eyes—blue, or melting point—350°c.). Entries can cross-refer to other entries both in the same file and in other files; in fact, values of attributes can be the names of entries elsewhere in the data base. At any point in these files, which are in technical language, plain language comments can be inserted.

Conversations relating to this data base are carried out by typewriter input and display screen output on-line to a computer doing batch-process work. This need not be related to the fact retrieval; most multiaccess computers are given background work such as payrolls, timetables, etc. to fill up their time. The conversations are limited to certain simple types, the two main ones being submission of new data (the user completes a sequence of forms on the screen by using the typewriter to add words to those already there), and question and answer. The typical answer to a question will consist of a sequence of displays (equivalent to pages) and the user can browse by sending "page-turning" commands.

Questions call for data to be selected from all entries satisfying criteria stated in the query. For example:
(1) Give date and place for all bank raids in the last six months

involving a man about 30 with black hair.

(2) Give daily production rate for all class F products with subassemblies made in Bristol.

(3) QN2 J. Jones. (This query will retrieve certain standard data for all men with this name.)

The program analyzing the queries uses a dictionary compiled for the particular application, containing all attribute names (phrases like "with — hair" or "made in —"), and all function words like "give," "list," and "or." Items not found in the dictionary are interpreted by the program as values or comments according to context.

Evidently the above example could be described as an order-analytical method, in which the user compared data with a mental order that he has generated in his own brain. When the reordered data from the data base are consistent with a hypothesis he has already formed, he takes special note of them, and tries to confirm the hypothesis with further queries and reordered data.

Fact Retrieval from any Data Base. A computer system called SIR—Semantic Information Retriever—was described by Bertram Raphael in a report labeled MAC-TR-2. It was a small part of a vast project of Massachusetts Institute of Technology known as MAC: Machine Aided Cognition and Multiple Access Computer Systems. The conversation on page 182 illustrates some of SIR's capabilities. Remarks preceded by *** were typed in by the user, and all other remarks were typed by the computer. Notice that the computer asks questions if it can specify the missing item of information necessary to answer the inquiry. The computer's frequent comment (I UNDERSTAND) is a signal that some new information has gone into its stores, not haphazardly but into a place from which it will be recalled to the computer's working area at the right stage in dealing with future questions.

The top two-thirds of the conversation are based on set inclusion, i.e. the inclusion of entire sets in other sets. The topmost line makes the computer (1) decide that the statement is about set inclusion, (2) prepare a store labeled "Boys" (if it has not yet got one) for the names of any boys it might later be told

(***. EVERY BOY IS A PERSON)
(I UNDERSTAND)

(***. A FINGER IS PART OF A HAND)
(I UNDERSTAND)

(***. EACH PERSON HAS TWO HANDS)
(THE ABOVE SENTENCE IS AMBIGUOUS ** PLEASE RE-PHRASE IT)

(***. THERE ARE TWO HANDS ON EACH PERSON)
(I UNDERSTAND)

(***. HOW MANY FINGERS DOES JOHN HAVE Q)
(THE ABOVE SENTENCE IS AMBIGUOUS ** BUT I ASSUME (HAS) MEANS (HAS AS PARTS))
(I DON*T KNOW WHETHER-FINGER IS PART OF JOHN)

(***. JOHN IS A BOY)
(I UNDERSTAND)

(***. HOW MANY FINGERS DOES JOHN HAVE Q)
(THE ABOVE SENTENCE IS AMBIGUOUS ** BUT I ASSUME (HAS) MEANS (HAS AS PARTS))
((HOW MANY FINGER PER HAND Q))

(***. EVERY HAND HAS 5 FINGERS)
(THE ABOVE SENTENCE IS AMBIGUOUS ** BUT I ASSUME (HAS) MEANS (HAS AS PARTS))
(I UNDERSTAND)

(***. HOW MANY FINGERS DOES JOHN HAVE Q)
(THE ABOVE SENTENCE IS AMBIGUOUS ** BUT I ASSUME (HAS) MEANS (HAS AS PARTS))
(THE ANSWER IS 10)

(***. HOW MANY AUTOMOBILES DOES JOHN HAVE Q)
(THE ABOVE SENTENCE IS AMBIGUOUS ** PLEASE RE-PHRASE IT)

(***. WHO IS PRESIDENT OF THE UNITED STATES Q)
(STATEMENT FORM NOT RECOGNIZED)

(***. THE BOY IS JUST TO THE LEFT OF THE TABLE)
(G02840 IS A TABLE)
(I UNDERSTAND)

(***. THE LAMP IS JUST TO THE LEFT OF THE TABLE)
(G02841 IS A LAMP)
(THE ABOVE STATEMENT IS IMPOSSIBLE)

(***. THE TABLE IS TO THE RIGHT OF THE CHAIR)
(G02842 IS A CHAIR)
(I UNDERSTAND)

(***. WHAT IS THE RELATIVE POSITION OF A PERSON Q)
(THE LEFT-TO-RIGHT ORDER IS AS FOLLOWS)
(CHAIR (BOY TABLE))

about, (3) prepare a similar store labeled "Persons," and (4) make a note in some way of the fact that every member of the first set is automatically a member of the second set; this is done by making an entry in the store for Persons, requiring that whenever a list of all Persons is sent to the working area of the computer, a list of all Boys must also be included with it.

Not that the computer generates all its answers by simply consulting lists. Its more interesting work comes under the category of *theorem proving* (a branch of mathematical logic), which uses a number of principles discovered mainly in the 1930s and 1960s. These lead to efficient procedures for testing the truth of statements about even very large sets of objects, given that a collection of simpler statements are true. This is the sort of development that Asa Kasher would consider to be premature: by his example opposite, Raphael showed that, although SIR made a true and relevant reply, it was not at that time capable of formulating and proving the statement required. But, however far the mathematicians can go in producing sophisticated fact-retrieval systems, we are concerned with how they will be used. There is evidence that systems such as the police example will have wide application.

We must now consider the points of similarity between the three examples of scientific discovery by order analysis and the two examples of fact retrieval. In all five cases there is a data base from which inferences are to be drawn—without the possibility of experimental checks at that time. Inferences are drawn by asking questions of the data base, one after the other, until an answer emerges that gives an encouraging lead. More specific questions are then asked until all useful information on this particular lead has been extracted. From the overall similarity it seems likely that any way of using computers in fact retrieval is also a possible way of using them in order analysis. Clearly the three scientific investigations would have had an easier passage if their data had been in core stores instead of books, and the questions had been asked through suitable fact-retrieval systems.

We may look forward to new scientific investigations, using data bases too big to be managed by human effort alone, and perhaps to new questioning techniques derived from the non-scientific applications of fact retrieval. Surely it is reasonable to expect such developments, leading to a harvest of new scientific discoveries. They are likely to be most numerous in the less experimental sciences such as astrophysics, geophysics, medicine, language, economics, political science, sociology, history, archaeology, agriculture, plant pathology, epidemiology, and also psychology.

At the time of writing there are about a dozen research projects in fact retrieval for special purposes, including in their data bases police information, health, pharmacology, insurance, taxation, stocks and shares, law, and social activities. All data bases such as these, which derive from real life, are for the present intended for the modest purpose of question answering, on-line to the computer. The operator does the thinking and asks the primary questions. His system provides the answers in a few seconds and saves him the delaying, distracting job of switching his attention to document files, and reading unwanted material before he finds what he wants. Without a computerized system he might easily fail to overcome the distractions and to complete his investigation; certainly he would work more slowly and get less done.

Typically, the operator will use his fact-retrieval system for a short series of order analyses, by means of which he will "size up the situation." He will thereby reach a decision requiring action, for which he will go outside the system to question a witness, write a letter, consult a colleague, or do whatever he deems necessary. In any sort of action he is in reality trying out some hypothesis, making a controlled experiment. He may even say to himself, "I'll try this idea on Green," "I'll see whether a letter will help; it can't do any harm." He is therefore behaving exactly like the experimental scientist who is in a position to perform a causal-analytical experiment.

If question answering systems are good for business execu-

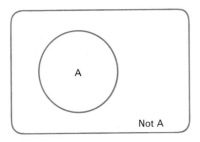

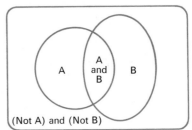

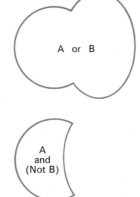

These diagrams illustrate the effect of the logical operations AND, OR, and NOT. They describe some of the steps taken by the programmer or occurring in the hardware of the computer. In practice they happen in both areas of activity, but for different purposes.

tives, almost axiomatically they will be good for scientists, but so far there has been no strong move toward enlisting them in scientific research. This may at first seem odd, because the scientists were the first to enlist the aid of computers and the business people followed. The general-purpose digital computer, when it came, was both a highly attractive toy and a refined instrument with untold applications. Mathematicians had to probe its capabilities, and some of them spent time in programming it for such purposes as playing noughts and crosses, chequers, and chess—it was all part of the great question: is the brain like a digital computer and, if not, what is it like? But it was obvious from the start that hitherto hopeless mathematical problems could now be solved by "numerical analysis," and also that a great deal of tedious processing observations could be taken over by computers. Commercial uses of computers for even more tedious data processing— payroll, finance, stock control, and other clerical work— developed rapidly and stimulated manufacturers to go on producing bigger and better computers.

Nonnumerical applications of computers advanced more slowly although it was realized from the beginning that the components of computers were performing logical operations (AND, OR, NOT) on the sets of binary digits they were handling—indeed they soon came to be called "logic elements." Mathematicians again found themselves new things to do, developing dazzling theories of automata, semigroups, and combinatorial situations, and like earlier mathematical developments some of these will perhaps lead to commercial applications. The intellectual approach to nonnumerical problems has certainly been influenced by computers, but it has not so far brought them new business.

Neither has it brought much help to those university faculties and others who might be using computers in order-analytical research. They can, of course, expect to benefit from the rapid progress still being achieved through the engineering-manufacturing approach. Computer manufacturers do extremely valuable research in the use of computers, and they expend a great deal of this effort on projects with no particular customer in mind. They are also quite accustomed, in their technical sales departments, to doing a great deal of any customer's hard thinking for him. But they have not yet produced any research results in, to them, unfamiliar fields of science with the help of computer-aided fact retrieval—nor are they likely to do so, because they lack basic training in these fields. The remoter university faculties, biased toward art rather than science, are still very tentative in their attitude to computers, and cannot be expected to start using them in ways that both mathematicians and engineers have avoided. There is also the problem of capital investment in any data base large enough for order-analytical research. Such a data base must be large, for any useful results provable with a small amount of data have probably already been proved manually. It must therefore be expensive, and making data bases is not a suitable occupation for the young graduates most likely to use them.

It is easy to find reasons for the comparative backwardness of fact retrieval, and it is in any case only slight tardiness in comparison with the very rapid general advancement of data processing. On the other hand, there are no good reasons why fact retrieval should not advance in its turn and become a cherished maid-of-all-work for everyone in need of order-analytical data processing. The coming era of multiaccess computing will help a good deal, by (a) making expensive data bases accessible to a larger number of inquirers, and (b) allowing on-line question-answering; so that it will be worth people's while to ask questions that have never been asked before. Some of these questions will be worth the proverbial 64,000 dollars, and this is one reason among many others why the great rush of new scientific discoveries that this century has witnessed seems likely to continue unabated.

As to information retrieval, it includes some rather awkward, nonnumerical tasks that we should like to unload on the computer. We do them ourselves, rather badly, and should be grateful if computers would do them even slightly more effectively than we can. The important thing is to start, without making a false start, because from then on the computer's help will grow substantially.

Suggested Reading

H. E. Barnes, *A History of Historical Writing*, Dover (New York, 1962)

J. Becker, R. M. Hayes, *Information Storage and Retrieval*, John Wiley (New York, 1963)

R. G. Colodny (Ed.), *Frontiers of Science and Philosophy*, Allen and Unwin (London, 1967)

C. Cuadra (Ed.), *Annual Review of Information Science and Technology*, Interscience (New York, 1966, 1967, 1968)

D. Diringer, *Writing*, Thames and Hudson (London, 1962) Praeger (New York, 1962)

R. A. Fairthorne, *Towards Information Retrieval*, Butterworth and Co. (Toronto, 1961)

D. O. Hebb, *The Organisation of Behavior*, John Wiley (New York, 1949) Chapman and Hall (London, 1950)

M. Kochen (Ed.), *The Growth of Knowledge*, John Wiley (New York, London, 1967)

B. Kyle, *Teach Yourself Librarianship*, English University Press (London, 1964)

J. C. R. Licklider, *Libraries of the Future*, Massachusetts Institute of Technology Press (Massachusetts, 1968)

W. C. B. Sayers, *An Introduction to Library Classification*, Grafton and Co., (9th Edit. London, 1954)

C. E. Shannon and W. Weaver, *The Mathematical Theory of Communication*, University of Illinois Press (Illinois, 1949)

A. M. Weinberg (Chairman), *Science, Government, and Information*. A report to the President's Science Advisory Committee. The White House (Washington, January 10th, 1963)

N. Wiener, *Ex Prodigy: My Childhood and Youth*, Simon and Schuster (New York, 1953) Book Centre (London, 1964)

Picture Credits

8 Photo Colin G. Butler, F.R.P.S.: 13 Nick Lucas: 18 Black Star, New York/ Photo E. Tamiso: 22 (Top) after D. O. Hebb, *The Organization of Behavior*, John Wiley & Sons, Inc., New York; (Bottom) after J. Z. Young, *A Model of the Brain*, Oxford University Press, by permission of the author: 24 Photo Roger Hyde © Aldus Books: 25 Photo Graham Finlayson: 28 Courtesy John Crossley & Sons Ltd.: 32 Photo Layton Sun Ltd. © Aldus Books. By courtesy of the Science Museum, London: 33 IBM World Trade Corporation: 35 after Allan Fletcher, ed. *Computer Science for Management*, Business Publications, Ltd., London:

190

Index _{Page numbers in *italics* refer to illustrations}

Dartmouth College, New Hampshire, 144
data communication, 156–67; public network of, 124–5, 157–63, *160*, 167; use by libraries of, 163–7
de Grolier, Eric, 95
de Sallo, Denis, 113–4
descriptors: in alphabetical indexing, 104; in faceted classification, 92–4, *93*, *94*; machine-generated, *108*, 110–1
Dewey, Melvil, 88
Diringer, Dr. David, 58, 60, 62
discussion: importance in current awareness of, 118, *119*
documentation, 117, 126–7

East, H., 72
electronic: computer, *see* computer; counters, 39–40, *40*; stores, *see* stores
electronics: definition of, 37
Elias, A. W., 102
evaluation of retrieval systems, 128–34

fact retrieval, 171–87; computerized, *169*, 174, 179–87, *183*
Fairthorne, R. A., 97
Fédération Internationale de Documentation, 94
ferrites, 45–6
Fisher, R. A., 176
Francis, Sir Frank, 135

Hebb, D. O., 21
Hertzsprung, E., 177; *see also* order analysis
hole punches: electronic, 50–1; hand, 34; machine, 34
hole sensing: definition of, 34; brush, *32*, 34; electronic, *48*, 49–50; pneumatic, 34–5, *36*; push-rod, *29*, 31, 34, *35*
Hollerith: card, *32*, 33–4; Herman, 33; machines, 33–4; tabulator, 32
hybrid computers, *see* computers

indexing, 101–111; alphabetical, 104, 106–7; citation, 101–3; cyclic title (KWIC), 102–4, 107; optical coincidence, *105*, 106–7

information: centers, 70–2, 77–8, 166; formula for noise-free channel, 14; formula for noisy channel, 131; process, 75; theory, 12–4
Institute for Scientific Information, USA, 121–2
Institution of Electrical Engineers, London, *116*, 121, 125

Jacquard: Joseph, *29*, 31; loom, *29*, 31, 34
Journal des Sçavans, *113*, 114
journals: importance of in current awareness, 114–8

Kasher, Asa, 179, 183
Kennedy, John F., 74
keywords: in classification and indexing, 102–11, *108*
Kochen, Manfred, 179
Kushul, A. Y., 102
Kyle, Barbara, 70

language, 21, 57–8
libraries: of 2000 B.C., 62; part played by scientific, 118–24
library: classification systems *see* classification; definition of, 63–4; lending, *57*, 67–9, *68*; services, 70, 76–8; work of, *57*
Library of Congress, 65, *65*, 75, 89
Licklider, J. C. R., 99
line printer, *50*, 51, 149
Liston, David, M., 71

magnetic: disks, *44*, 45, 48, 90; drums, 44–5, *44*, 48, 90; tape, 42–5, *44*, 48; stores, *see* stores
magnetostriction, 41
Martyn, J., 72
Massachusetts Institute of Technology, 181
MATPS at Yale University Library, 69–70, *73*
memory, 20–7, *22;* folk, *25*, 26; long-term, 21; short-term, 20–1
Mendeleeff, D. I., 174–6, *175*, 177; *see also* order analysis
Metal Box Company, 95
microfiches, 107, 114